AF469440

Guns and Goshawks

GUNS and GOSHAWKS

COUNTRY LIFE AND COUNTRY SPORTS

Richard Brigham

Illustrated by Alan Langford

BLANDFORD PRESS
LONDON NEW YORK SYDNEY

First published in the UK 1988 by Blandford Press,
an imprint of Cassell Publishers Limited,
Artillery House, Artillery Row, London SW1P 1RT

Distributed in the United States by
Sterling Publishing Co, Inc,
2 Park Avenue, New York, NY 10016

Distributed in Australia by
Capricorn Link (Australia) Pty Ltd
PO Box 665, Lane Cove, NSW 2066

British Library Cataloguing in Publication Data

Brigham, R.J. (Richard J.)
Guns and goshawks : country life and
country sports.
1. England. Rural regions. Social life —
Personal observations
I. Title
942.085′8′0924
ISBN 0 7137 2041 7

Typeset by Inforum Ltd, Portsmouth

Printed and bound in Great Britain by
Mackays of Chatham PLC, Chatham, Kent

Contents

Beware of the Boy

It is now difficult for me to recall my initiation into the world of country pursuits, but I am reliably informed that it all began on the grand occasion of my sixth birthday when, amongst a hoard of other juvenile treasures, I discovered the very desirable and long-awaited gift of a new popgun.

To my undiscerning eye it was doubtless a splendid weapon, despite the fact that it possessed an extremely restricted range. Corks somewhat grudgingly ejected were fastened to a ring at the muzzle end by three feet of binder twine, thus preventing the wholesale loss of reusable ammunition. Nevertheless, despite the obvious shortcomings of my first weapon, the initial smoulderings of a strong flame had been ignited and I rather fancied myself in the role of big game hunter. To my tender and inexperienced self the gleaming weapon appeared to fulfil all the necessary requirements of the well-equipped and self-respecting marksman.

My quarry – which could now only be entered under the 'various' column of the game book – was quite easily stalked around the confines of our large country garden and a row of adjoining tumbledown stables, as at the time my parents kept a wide variety of livestock to aid with the task of making a living from the land. A motley assortment of pigs, chickens, cockerels and other lesser domestic fry were continually subjected to my early hunting instincts, and it was not unusual for a recumbent pig or unsuspecting fowl to discover itself on the receiving end of the offensive cork. Nothing was safe for long. Regardless of the discomfort inflicted upon my victims, the spate of corking continued until our so-called domesticated stock became semi-domesticated and of a highly nervous disposition. They grew considerably wilder and more evasive and eventually turned the tables by resorting to retaliatory measures. It was only when I had succeeded in putting the hens off the lay, taken numerous trouncings from Hitler the highstepping cockerel and finally been ousted from the piggery by an irate Large White sow that I considered it prudent to turn my attentions to less vengeful, though wilier, prey.

In particular I turned to the large resident sparrow population always to be found raiding father's vegetable garden. I recall vast legions of house sparrows basking happily in the sun on the moss-covered roof slates of our house, apparently completely unafraid – or completely oblivious – of the potential dangers that lurked below. Taking a positive bead on any that were foolish enough to remain on the ridge tiles, with great deliberation I shut my eyes and pulled the trigger, thus releasing the cork on its short trajectory with what seemed like a colossal explosion. Then, almost beside myself with excitement, I dropped the gun and raced to the back of the house to see if I had been lucky.

Needless to say I soon tired of this, as the game larder was permanently empty, and to cap it all the cork, sailing true until arrested by the length of binder twine, had the most painfully annoying habit of whipping back to collide with some tender region of my anatomy. The top of my head was a favoured target with, as a close second, directly behind my left ear. I became

afraid of inflicting far greater damage upon myself than to intended victims and had already begun to suspect that there was at least some measure of truth in the label of 'bloodsportsman' with which sporting folk are frequently branded by those ignorant of the country way of life.

My earliest foray in the hunting field sticks vividly in my mind. Playing alone in father's mealshed one morning, I happened to spot what looked to me like a large brown mouse scampering around inside one of the tall metal tubs of pig meal, obviously trapped and unable to scale the slippery sides of the bin. I called mother to come and have a look, but as usual she was busy with the household duties and failed to put in an appearance. Not wishing her to miss out on my discovery I decided to capture the 'mouse' and take it indoors where she could give it a more detailed examination. With great difficulty I managed to seize hold of the long, scaly tail as the beast revolved with ever-increasing speed around the tub. I hoisted it unceremoniously from its prison, but immediately dropped the ungrateful rodent as it twisted to leave a neat set of teethmarks on the ball of my thumb as a gesture of its appreciation. Fearing repercussions, my new-found friend bolted rapidly out of the shed door and along the garden path towards the house. Hot on its heels and wielding father's pigstick I managed to herd it skilfully through the open back door and into the living room, where mother was busy on her hands and knees scrubbing the floor.

'Here he comes, mummy', I exclaimed with glee, 'it's a *lovely* big mouse!'

Upon reflection it was not surprising that mother was not particularly overjoyed at the prospect of sharing her living quarters with a huge doe rat, however lovely, but before she could halt our combined progress the rat had skidded past her across the wet flagstones and disappeared into a convenient crack behind the piano, from whence it turned to inspect the pair of us in more detail before deciding upon its next course of action. A pair of black beady eyes set behind a whisker-twitching snout kept watch as mother delivered a well-deserved lecture on the impracticalities of housing a pet rat, then rushed outside to the kennel to collect Floss, our liver and white cocker spaniel, to evict the squatter.

The old dog waited at the mouth of the crack while the piano was shifted, tail gently wagging in anticipation of the rat's next move. There was no move. Floss was far too large to force an entry into the rodent's hide-out and the rat itself was certainly not budging voluntarily. Sensing something of an anticlimax, I administered to the rat a helpful prod in the ribs with the pigstick, causing it to pop out with the speed of a champagne cork between the old dog's legs. The chase was on! The ensuing battle on the hearthrug showed me how quickly and effectively a dog can reduce a rat to a lifeless and mat-staining mess in a matter of seconds. I remained unpopular for the rest of the day.

But despite the dangers, mishaps and failures of the early days the instincts grew within me and it was not long before I was in search of a more successful fowling piece to replace the inefficiencies of the popgun. I was not old enough and certainly too inexperienced to be allowed the responsibilities of a firearm, and so was forced to resort to that first weapon so beloved of all young country boys — and so despised by those living in close proximity — the catapult. I made one myself with the outlay of a few hard-earned pence for a suitable length of square rubber. A young ash sapling was carefully fashioned to form the forked grip that held one end of the rubber straps, and a small leather thong was bound tightly to the business end to hold the loaded missiles. Now the sparrows were for it! But *passer domesticus* continued to thrive on the roof of the house, although a large number of brittle tiling slates were less fortunate, suffering heavy losses beneath an unrelenting barrage of inaccurate pebbles. Luckily I improved with practice and after long, arm-tiring sessions became quite adept at shattering the small white insulators supporting the telephone cables that ran past our garden. When these had been sufficiently thinned out, and as I feared repercussions from the General Post Office, I decided that it was high time to concentrate my efforts on the wild game of the countryside.

I began to explore my potential hunting grounds carefully. Our house and garden were part of a small Norfolk village set in the very heart of the countryside; a dozen weatherworn cottages nestled cosily along the base of a broad undulating river valley. On three sides the village was guarded by gently rolling hills and along the fourth, the northern aspect, flowed the silver snake of the River Wensum as it twisted on its path, ambling slowly and peacefully among the lush, cattle-grazed water meadows that line its route to the city of Norwich. From there its waters emerge to continue the journey through the vast windmill-lined flatlands towards Great Yarmouth and the open sea.

The valley itself consisted of a maze of small fields, each divided from its neighbour by a network of thick hedgerows of thorn and hazel, studded with gnarled, ivy-clad oaks and towering elms, standing like a proud regiment of guards against the power of the four winds. The entire valley was literally alive with enthralling things to occupy any small boy's mind, a veritable birdwatcher's, angler's and sportsman's paradise. It was indeed little wonder that I developed a great interest in the seemingly endless procession of natural beauty that lived on my doorstep, and later nurtured a desire for skill and knowledge in the ways of harvesting some of the surplus nature provided.

Father worked long hours on the family farm, but sometimes found time to set out with his twelve-bore to supplement the cooking pot with the odd pheasant or rabbit. On rare occasions I was allowed to accompany him around the fields and marshes in the dewy, misty, tree-dripping half-light of dawn, eyes and ears constantly alert for any signs of game and nostrils tingling with the sweet and exciting smell of burnt gunpowder. I wanted so much to be allowed the privilege of carrying a gun, but had to content myself with the lesser powers of the catapult.

In fact, although I failed to appreciate it at the time, by virtue of its diminutive powers the catapult taught me much of the art of stalking and woodcraft and opened up a whole new and fascinating vista. Among the hedgerows, fields and meadows resided a boundless wealth of birds and beasts to be observed, marvelled at or stalked, each according to its own elusive powers or edible qualities. Although actual bags were small and indeed virtually nonexistent there was always some new sight or sound to awaken interest, some secret undiscovered place to explore and always the chance, albeit a very slender one, of returning home triumphantly with something for the pot.

I well remember bagging my very first pheasant with the faithful catty. On my daily wanderings around the farm I had stalked and taken potshots at innumerable pheasants, many of which I almost knew by name, so frequent had been my attempts towards a more intimate relationship. The pheasants too, it seemed, were beginning to accustom themselves to the almost daily ritual of being showered with whizzing marbles – for such was my ammunition – probably looking upon it as a necessary evil to be endured until my arms grew tired and they were allowed to glean the corn stubbles in peace again. The nearest I had ever come to slaying my first pheasant was one foggy morning when, more by good luck than judgement, I rolled over a splendid old cock as he stood preening the early morning dew from his finery on the top of a stook of straw bales. My elation was short lived, however, for even as I ran to pick him up he rather shakily took to his wings, skimming all too healthily across the acres of golden stubble and suffering nothing greater than the very mildest form of concussion.

On the evening of the first pheasant bag I had been pottering around the cattle pastures close to home, unproductively terrorising the inhabitants of a small rabbit warren on the banks of an old marl working. The gathering gloom of dusk was just beginning to close in around me, veiling the distant woods in a thin blue-grey mist, when suddenly I spotted her; a single hen pheasant strutting boldly towards her roosting place in a belt of bushy elms that formed the centre of a long and tangled hedgerow. I watched, excited but with unaccustomed patience, as the bird, after making a long, reassuring study of her immediate surroundings, flapped awkwardly to a prominent branch 20 feet above the ground. There, after much shuffling and rousing and an interminable preening of feathers, she eventually settled herself for the coming of night. Being of an uncooperative nature the bird had chosen an obvious vantage point as her nocturnal resting place. To stand any chance of getting her I would need to cross a wide stretch of open ground, almost inevitably putting her to flight before a suitably comfortable marbling range could be achieved. But a plan began to form . . .

Much later that night I went to work on father as he sat toasting himself in front of a blazing coal fire after the evening meal. A plump and tender pheasant, I informed him, would be a welcome addition to our diet and could be easily secured. This was a chance far too good to miss. Father was not entirely

convinced but eventually, more by way of keeping the peace than with any serious expectations of a good free meal, he reluctantly agreed to accompany me as torchbearer into the nose-tingling sharpness of a frosty night.

We arrived beneath the tree with a strong torch, the catapult and a pocketful of the ubiquitous glass alleys. After stumbling amongst a twisted jungle of tree roots at the base of the elms, our systematic search of the high branches revealed the hen, sitting precariously astride a slender bough almost at the top of the tree, swaying gently to and fro, in a light breeze that pushed cotton-wool clouds across a three-quarter moon. As father held the torch steady I unsuccessfully loosed marble after marble at the stubborn bird. Reds, blues, greens and purples; all were to no avail. Our prospective dinner was not to be taken easily. It obstinately refused to drop dead, or for that matter even budge. It merely looked alarmed, croaked indignantly and shook its head when hit.

Eventually father and I – not to mention the pheasant – grew tired of this and, fitting a heavy three-quarter inch bolt from the bottom of my trouser pocket into the leather thong, I summoned all my reserves of strength and hauled back the heavy rubber as far as my short arms would allow. The resulting missile sped fast and true under its increased power, catching the luckless bird directly under the beak and knocking it unceremoniously from the perch it had shown so much reluctance to leave. As it flapped earthwards through the tangle of branches in the darkness, it had the misfortune to fall almost on top of father, who grabbed it as it flapped between his legs. Success at last! My school cap would never fit again. It was a proud hunter that returned to our house that night, excited and trembling hands firmly clutching the still warm body of his first pheasant. To me that pheasant tasted far superior to any that I had previously eaten. From that moment on, woe betide any tin can, pop bottle or marauding neighbour's cat that strayed into my domain.

Fruitful expeditions in the hunting field became much more frequent following the discovery of a free and lethal supply of ammunition. I spotted, mixed with the granite chippings used for surfacing the road, many small lumps of iron embedded in a coating of sticky tar. The only method of securing this almost unlimited supply of projectiles involved the rather tiresome and often risky task of chipping holes in the surface of the road around each piece in order to prise it out with an iron bar; thus our already bumpy road became even more pot-holed and uneven after each collecting session. The clinging deposit of tar was an unvoidable nuisance, as my trouser pockets were frequently gummed up with the gooey substance, but for all this the lumps sped with positively lethal results upon anything that was foolish enough to linger in their path of flight. Unfortunately they did not always fly true, as at first I possessed a far greater degree of enthusiasm than of accuracy.

I was encouraged to take up fishing, a quiet, peacefully absorbing pastime in which I presented much less of a public – though more of a personal – liability with the rod than I did with the catapult. I needed very little persuasion. The River Wensum flowed throughout the entire length of the farm, its waters clear and sparkling during dry spells but murky and clouded in times of flood. It provided a constant source of wonder and delight, its gentle flow giving a home to a multitude of wild and beautiful creatures. Beneath the mirrored surface on which the water skater and the whirligig beetle spun dizzily during the hot summer months, fat, red-finned roach and rudd glided lazily in the gravelly shallows, accompanied by sleek, quicksilver shoals of wandering dace. The seemingly bottomless holes at every bend, choked and shaded by clumps of weaving weed, held the boldly striped perch, the sinuous eel and that savage killer, the pike. I spent many happy hours on the lush river banks, the scent of crushed water mint heavy in my nostrils, fishing rod in hand and eyes mesmerised by a little red float bobbing gently on the surface.

My sister Pamela, with whom I normally shared something of a cat-and-dog relationship, was my elder by three years. She also took an interest in fishing, especially as it all too often allowed her the welcome opportunity of outdoing her younger brother. Due to our tender years we were not officially allowed within casting distance of the river unattended, a harsh though not unjust safety precaution in view of the fact that we both had a marked tendency to fall in, down or off any even remotely dangerous obstacle encountered on our travels. Thus it was necessary for us to persuade mother or father to accompany us on fishing expeditions. Each and every Sunday afternoon during the season, parental after-dinner slumbers would be interrupted by a pair of begging and pleading would-be anglers and there was little peace until we were on our way, loaded up with a considerable and largely unnecessary burden of rods, nets and vast assortments of tackle boxes and tins of writhing maggots and worms. If for some reason our combined efforts failed to provide an escort we pretended to give in, but made quite sure that we paraded our equally long and miserable faces well in sight of father, hoping to appeal to his compassionate nature. This ruse generally had the desired effect and off we would go to renew acquaintance with the world of buzzing bees, darting dragonflies and hawking swallows, and, we hoped, with the shoals of elusive silver fish.

There was but one cloud on my horizon. My favourite stretch of the river bank, beneath which lay gathered ranks of roach, perch, dace and gudgeon, was densely overhung by an umbrella-like growth of interwoven branches, trailing almost to water level from a stand of tall ash trees that provided shade and shelter for the denizens of the river. During the heat of the summer afternoons large shoals of roach and dace would arrive at my lie from the shallower regions to spend the remainder of the hot hours in the cooler, leaf-dappled waters almost at my feet. Overcome by the thrill of seeing hordes of fish queuing up for my unlimited worm supply, the accuracy of my casting out sadly deteriorated and it was seldom long before I succeeded in hooking one or other of the low-lying branches.

Prompted by loud though scientifically quite inaccurate descriptions of ash trees, father would eventually arrive on the scene to enquire calmly which branch I had managed to catch this time. After retrieving my tackle he would wander off to keep watch from a safe distance just out of hook range, knowing only too well that he would be called upon again in the not too distant future to carry out an identical operation, for a few casts later invariably found me in the same infernal muddle. How I hated those ash trees!

Big sister, who was content to remain on the more open and less obstructed reaches of the bank, was much amused by my antics; but I eventually had the last laugh one afternoon when, more by a bit of good luck than through any fishing skill, she somehow managed to fasten her hook into the gaping jaws of what to us seemed like a huge pike. It all happened quite unexpectedly. Fishing in midstream with a bait of rolled bread, her float suddenly dipped below the surface and she was into quite a fair-sized roach. The captive splashed and fought as she rather clumsily played it towards the shallows near the bank, but before she could haul it from the water with the usual ceremonious sneer in my direction, there was an almighty splash as a ravenous pike darted from a weed bed and promptly gobbled it up!

To my delight it gave Pamela the fright of her life, causing her to jump up and down on the bank, stricken with terror and undecided whether to hang on, drop the rod or scream for help. Leaping about like a demented grasshopper did nothing whatever to ease the situation, for the pike, no doubt equally terrified, proceeded to put as great a distance between itself and its reluctant captor as possible, screaming the line from her reel at a considerable rate of knots and hurtling rapidly downstream in the general direction of the North Sea. Luckily for Pamela two things happened in rapid succession: the pike decided to turn back before her line had run out and father rushed to the rescue with the landing net, somehow succeeding in slipping it beneath the still very lively fish as Pamela cautiously reeled it back into the shallows.

After a fierce and frantic struggle on both sides the pike finally

lay gasping on the grassy bank, a savage grey-green monster of a few pounds, its colours seeming to reflect my feelings. My bag of four ash branches, one bed of stinging nettles and a brace of four-inch gudgeons paled into insignificance against the gleaming leviathan. I consoled myself by informing Miss Clever Dick that father had done all the hard work; she had merely held the rod and even that menial task had left her in a state of extreme shock. Needless to say, her capture of the pike and the resulting smug expression she wore for days afterwards did nothing to strengthen the tenuous thread on which our mutual regard was delicately suspended.

I later evolved a far easier though possibly less sporting way of extracting pike from the river. Using a springy ten foot bamboo rod, I wired a rabbit snare to one end, fully enlarging the noose to form a perfect circle which could be slipped over the head of any unsuspecting fish that lay basking in the shallows or at the mouth of drainage channels. Once the technique of gauging underwater depth and distance was finally mastered, this most simple of tools proved its worth many times over. In order not to alarm the fish, pole and wire were slipped carefully into the water well upstream of where it lay and allowed to drift downstream, keeping exact pace with the current to avoid a telltale ripple on the surface. If depth and distance had been correctly ascertained, the open noose could be slipped delicately over the tapered snout until it passed the gently pulsating gills. An upward wrench to tighten the wire and the pike was mine. A few more young duck, coot and grebes would be spared to grow to maturity, safe from the submerged attacks of this most ruthless of freshwater killers.

My favourite type of fishing was for perch, that boldly striped, scarlet-finned glutton of the deep holes and weedy regions of the river. At that time it was one of the most common and easily caught species, and it was not long before I discovered that the fish were very good to eat. Father arrived home from work one evening to find me busy on the front doorstep with a rusty penknife, dressing out a perch of a pound and a half taken that afternoon on a minnow. I had made rather a mess of gutting and filleting the fish, and the end result looked far from appetising, being liberally smeared with soil, blades of grass and the odd cat's hair or two for good measure.

'You're never going to eat that thing!', was his only comment as he stepped over the mess to get indoors; but it was quite a different story a few minutes later when I had it sizzling away merrily in the frying pan. The aroma from the blackened morsels smelled really delicious, and it proved to be one of the tastiest fish I had ever eaten. Even father had to agree when he rather hesitantly sampled a portion. I had discovered another regular source of natural food, as perch were quite readily taken on a lobworm or minnow.

To make really certain of fast results I invented a sure-fire method, which involved the use of a home-made minnow trap. At that time a minnow trap was an important part of almost every young country boy's possessions, and a really effective model could be made from an empty wine bottle – the type that had a funnel-like inversion in its base. The end of the funnel had to be very carefully removed, leaving a small hole by which the minnows could gain access. A piece of thin string was threaded through the hole and out at the neck and tied together outside, and a length was left attached for tethering it to the bank. Corked at the top end, the trap could be filled with bread crusts and lowered into the shallows where minnows shoaled in numbers, and it was not long before there were a dozen or so inside, unable to find the way out.

The bottle was then hauled out of the shallows and gently

lowered into one of the dark holes where perch were known to congregate, and when returning to fish a few hours later sport would be fast and furious. Having spotted the minnows inside the bottle, a great shoal of perch would be lining up and bumping their noses against the glass trying to get at the fish inside. After a couple of frustrating hours of this they were ready to snap at anything. It was but a simple matter to lower a hooked minnow within reach of the jar; it would be snapped up without hesitation by the ravenous perch, driven almost to distraction by the sight of an apparently easy but inaccessible meal. A little unsporting perhaps, but it worked like a dream.

Tricks of this nature were often employed in one form or another in catching other species of fish, and I found them especially lethal to the resident brown trout of the fast-flowing gravelly stretches of the Wensum. One such area lies beneath a stand of ancient oaks overhanging the river, and during the sweltering days of full summer a few wild brownies are always to be found in the cooler leaf-dappled waters on favoured lies. I found them rather elusive at first when I was using more conventional tactics, but soon learned to get the better of them with the minnow bottle or by pre-feeding them with maggots.

A week or so prior to fishing a dead pigeon or rabbit was tied to a branch hanging just upstream of where the trout lay in the shallows, and following a few hot days the body was soon crawling with maggots. After these had duly grown, a steady stream of them would fall into the water below, to be readily snapped up once the fish had acquired a taste for them. A couple of days of this and it became second nature for the trout to take them as soon as they hit the water. Fishing from a horizontal branch above them by dapping a maggot on the water invariably met with success, although it was far from easy to play a lively wild trout from such a precarious position. If a larger than normal fish was hooked I had to drop ten feet or so into the water; but as it was summer, getting soaked to the skin in the process of landing the fish seemed well worth the reward.

At long last, having been denied the use of a real gun until I was believed to be ready and capable enough to be trusted with such a dangerous object, the great day arrived and I became the proud if diminutive owner of a brand new air rifle, a .177 calibre made by British Small Arms. The gun came complete with telescopic sight, a tin of pellets and a large supply of paper targets, although the latter remained unused. I could provide targets in any quantity. There were rabbits galore on the cattle pastures, wood pigeons in the trees and copses and a great many pheasants strutting all too freely about the golden corn stubbles, fearing little worse than an inaccurate hail from the thong of a worn-out catapult. Closer at hand, hordes of sparrows pilfered the kitchen garden and the hens' run, and an alarming number of rats had moved into the stables, raiding pig troughs, spreading filth and disease and generally causing damage by their persistent gnawing of the woodwork.

With the gun I acquired some new friends. Arthur, a retired countryman who had moved in next door, had spent some considerable part of his younger years in the service of His Majesty's armed forces, and upon seeing the gun immediately elected himself to be my military advisor. Thus I was religiously taught to 'Bear arms', 'Present arms' and 'Fire!', though I failed to appreciate what earthly use such commands would be when in pursuit of game, which gave little time or opportunity for such niceties. Arthur was rather deaf, which gave him the tendency to speak loudly, his normal tone of conversation being distinctly audible at something approaching three hundred yards. After drilling me with a verbal onslaught as loud and threatening as a regimental sergeant major's, Arthur often accompanied me in search of something for the pot. When a possible target was sighted I was immediately instructed to 'Present arms' and 'Fire!', a drill which may have served him well when confronted with a horde of screaming dervishes, but which failed miserably in the hunting field, causing even the bravest and deafest quarry to take to its wings or run for cover. Nonetheless we got on extremely well together and spent many happy hours roaming the normally peaceful fields and wild country lanes.

Our travels often took us past the home of another ancient country character. Herbert, a bewhiskered septuagenarian, resided alone in a tumbledown thatched cottage that had also seen better years, set in a large garden as thick and impenetrable as a jungle. Herbert quickly attained the position of something of a hero in my young eyes, for he had spent much of his three score and ten years with a gun tucked under his arm or, if the situation demanded a little discretion, hidden safely from view among the folds of a long overcoat. Herbert was invariably to be found leaning his meagre weight on the five-barred gate at the end of his path, puffing contentedly on a charred briar and emitting clouds of black, eye-stinging smoke that served as an effective insect repellent on the warm summer evenings. As if to compensate for his rather small stature, Herbert told some exceedingly tall tales and the very sight of the gun under my arm would send him back on countless reminiscences. I listened suitably wide-eyed and open-mouthed as the old character related a variety of sporting anecdotes, generally from the days of his father Jack who, Herbert assured me with a twinkle in his eye, had gained quite a reputation as a master poacher. I will never forget some of the tales he told me.

On one occasion in the far-off days of the muzzle-loading shotgun, old Jack was in the process of loading his gun one morning for a poaching foray, ramming home a wad of newspaper over the charge of powder with the ramrod. Pausing to look up, he was delighted to behold a flight of mallard winging directly over the corner of his garden, en route to a small pond nearby and flying in a perfectly straight formation. There was no time to load a charge of shot, so without further ado he primed his old fowling piece and fired the ramrod at the departing ducks. The ramrod described a graceful arc and fell heavily to earth, skewering no less than six duck together in its flight!

But this was only the beginning. Just by chance the duck happened to fall upon a covey of partridges that were dusting themselves in a close-knit bunch on a nearby stubble, killing all but one bird, which suffered no worse than a broken wing. Swift action was the order of the day. Abandoning his empty gun, old Jack sped hotfoot on the trail of the runner, on the way meeting with an extraordinary accident. Unbeknown to my hero a hare squatted concealed in her form amongst the stubble and Jack was tripped, killing her in the process and landing somewhat miraculously on top of another hare! When the complete bag was finally brought to hand, Jack's one and only shot had secured six duck, a complete covey of partridges and a brace of hares – quite a feat even for Herbert's vivid imagination to cope with.

Old Jack, it transpired, was a dab hand with the ramrod. On another of his murderous exploits he encountered a party of duck busily preening themselves on the thin branch of a willow tree overhanging the river just above water level. Taking careful and deliberate aim, he once again let fly with his trusty smokepole. The ramrod found its mark. Instead of aiming at the birds themselves, as would any normal but less enterprising fowler, Jack fired at the centre of the branch they were standing on, splitting it neatly down the middle with his usual precision. The rod's impact opened up a wide crack in the branch, but only momentarily, and when the two halves closed together they had trapped the ducks' webbed feet, rendering them completely helpless and able only to await collection at Jack's convenience.

Unfortunately it was necessary for the old fowler to cross the river in order to retrieve his bag. Plunging boldly into the icy waters, Jack set out to collect the results of yet another unique shot but – you've guessed it – he landed on a huge pike that had been minding its own business among a tangle of weed at the river-side. It promptly expired and floated to the surface. Returning laden with ducks and pike, Jack felt something squirming around in the interior of a wellington boot. Tipping it up when he returned to dry land, he found an eel inside, which had somehow mistaken the top of his boot for its river-bed retreat. Just to be on the safe side Jack emptied the other boot and, lo and behold, he had caught another. What a sportsman!

Even when rabbiting it was the same. One summer's evening a rabbit was spotted nibbling the grass beside the haystack behind which Jack hid. Not wishing to alarm it by appearing in full view around the edge of the stack, he bent his gun barrel around the corner and promptly bagged master rabbit. The recoil from the charge sent him sprawling backwards and, needless to relate, right on top of another luckless coney hiding in a bed of nettles behind him.

These and a great many other tales, tall as they may be, never failed to fill me with great amazement and, of course, envy at Jack's skills. Granted, I was often more than a trifle bewildered at some of the remarkable feats which seemed to form a great part of the old man's everyday life, but I believed them implicitly. And so in fact did Herbert, although the numbers involved had a habit of gradually ascending and distances multiplied regularly with each and every telling.

A Bird in the Hand

My initial flounderings in the ancient and exacting art of falconry were rather a hit and miss affair, which came about following the tragic and mysterious disappearance of a pair of nesting kestrels. I had discovered the nesting site in early spring, just after the pair first took up residence in an abandoned magpie's nest, high among the branches of an ivy-covered elm not far from our house. Following a few minor structural alterations to the dilapidated nest, a clutch of four, almost round, red-brown eggs were laid on the stout platform of twigs and roots and incubation commenced. For many days a considerable amount of my spare time was occupied in watching the adult birds, gloating over their eggs and falling down the tree — the last of these possibly the most frequent of my pastimes.

The eggs, or at least three of them, duly hatched. The fourth was probably infertile, remaining for a few days in the nest until its eventual dismissal over the edge. The tiny falcons, or eyases, were at first clothed in a buff white down and their rather grotesque and helpless appearance was increased by their large, heavy heads and oversized beaks. But after a few days the first stubby signs of feathers began to peep through the layer of fluffy down, and from then with the passing of each day a gradual transformation took place as the young birds almost imperceptibly assumed the slender lines of their parents.

The weeks of early summer marched steadily on. The adults were kept extremely busy throughout the daylight hours in a never-ending quest for food, journeying repeatedly to and from the nest to feed the trio of fast maturing offspring. Voles and shrews formed the main part of the diet, but disgorged pellets which I picked up below the tree were found on dissection to contain small feathers, apparently those of fledgeling birds, easy prey for such a swift and capable predator. The smaller male, or tiercel, appeared to perform the majority of the hunting duties, hovering continually over the close-cropped pastures and hay bottoms where prey could be easily located on the open ground. The female usually preferred to remain in close proximity to the nest, keeping a wary lookout for any threat of danger to her young and warding off the odd crow, jay or magpie that encroached on her domain.

But early one morning all was quiet at the nesting site. No anxious parent surveyed my approach along the hedgerow and when I walked towards the leaning elm a single magpie rose from its base, protesting loudly at being disturbed and vanishing quickly out of sight over a low belt of hazel fans. An eyas lay spreadeagled on the damp, dew-soaked grass, its bright eyes dulled, the body stiff and cold. I picked it up. Except for the partial loss of an eye there were no visible signs of injury. It had apparently died after falling from the nest during the night to the ground 30 feet below. The magpie was obviously not to blame as the body had already passed into rigor mortis and, had the magpie been the culprit, there would by this time have been few remains to tell the story.

Suddenly fearing for the safety of the rest of the brood I quickly scaled the old familiar mute-stained branches to the nest, where the two remaining youngsters huddled disconsolately, standing hunched together for mutual warmth and protection. The flattened nesting platform, stained with countless white mutes, looked cold and deserted. There were no traces of a fresh kill in the nest and the usual swarm of bluebottles were conspicuous by their absence. Not a scrap of meat remained to entice the bloated flies and they obviously sought elsewhere to deposit their burden of eggs. Many had already discovered the eyas below, for as I descended from the tree a veritable cloud buzzed back and forth above the lifeless corpse. Giving the deceased a decent burial away from the swarm of flies I pondered upon the fate of the adult hawks. Normally by this time one or other would be wheeling and swooping anxiously above me, 'kek-kekking' in alarm. Had they been shot, or trapped, or poisoned? It seemed incredible that both should disappear without trace within such a short period of time. But more important was the problem of what could be done to help the remaining youngsters.

With great reluctance I decided to leave the nesting site well alone for the remainder of the day, but to keep a watchful eye out in the direction of the elm in case the old birds should return. If they failed to reappear before nightfall to attend to feeding and brooding duties, the helpless youngsters would be in grave danger from the effects of cold and starvation during the long night, and added to this was the possible threat of nocturnal predators.

As the day wore on the skies around the nesting site remained ominously empty and it was soon quite clear that something was very wrong indeed. Some form of help was obviously called for and a plan of action gradually evolved in my mind.

During the heat of the afternoon I crouched concealed beneath the welcome shade of the henhouse, eventually toppling three house sparrows from its felted roof with the air rifle. I was unable to retrieve the result of my first shot, which fell almost upon the head of a particularly vicious looking hen and was promptly seized and carried off, its triumphant captor followed by a cluster of flapping and squawking hens all eager to share the tasty addition to their diet. I ensured the collection of numbers two and three by arming myself with a stout hazel stick, thus creating an even greater bout of flapping and squawking as rightful ownership was settled in no uncertain terms.

After minor preparations the half-light of dusk saw my arrival beneath the elm with a large cardboard box lined with a hessian sack. I had no glove with which to handle the potentially savage youngsters, but I hoped that, weakened by a foodless day, their fighting spirits would be considerably diminished and handling would present little difficulty.

But how wrong I was! As I reached into the nest for the nearest bird the quiet, inanimate forms suddenly transformed themselves into wild fighting machines as they spun to face me, laying back on stunted tails to rake my hand with needle-like talons. Wrapping the thick sleeve of my pullover around two bleeding fingers I eventually managed to transfer them, despite screaming protests,

safely into the confines of the box, closing the lid carefully with a sigh of relief. Darkness had almost fallen by the time I arrived home. The blue-grey mists of evening were gently rising from a backcloth of marshes where the plaintive cries of a lapwing, gyrating dizzily in the gloom, hung on the still night air. It was far too late for any attempt towards satisfying the hawks' appetites, but just in case I placed the plucked and jointed sparrows in one corner of the box within easy reach. I placed the box, its top covered with a heavy hessian sack, on an empty forage bin in one of the stables, leaving the birds to their own devices for the night.

The next morning I peered anxiously beneath the sack and was greatly relieved to find my charges apparently none the worse for their first night in captivity. To my surprise every trace of the food had vanished and both birds seemed to have regained much of their former strength and vigour, giving voice to ear-splitting threats and a rather competent display of their talon power as I looked down upon them. Their rich chestnut plumage, streaked and splashed with jet black brush strokes, now closely resembled that of the full-grown bird, for most of the delicate wisps of down had dropped from the feather tips. Their long yellow toes, tipped with black, curved spikes as sharp as needles, clung convulsively to the piece of sacking lining the base of their new nest as both pairs of eyes fixed me with a threatening stare.

It was abundantly clear that the birds could not be confined to the cardboard box much longer, and I immediately began the search for more spacious accommodation where they would be able to exercise their wings in preparation for the first flight. After weighing up the pros and cons I finally decided upon a larger lean-to shelter adjoining the row of stables. It already had a strong weatherproof roof of galvanised sheeting and three boarded sides, and it required little effort to add a wire netting front and to construct a perch or two in suitable places. By the end of the day I had finished. The wired front contained a small door at the edge to allow access and in the rear left-hand corner I had erected a platform of boards at shoulder height to serve as a feeding place, which would also accommodate the cardboard box until the hawks were old enough to use a perch for roosting.

As the days passed the hawks matured rapidly and in a relatively short space of time became agreeably docile and seemed completely confident in my presence. Appetites remained steady and I was kept extremely busy during my spare time to satisfy their continual demands. Unlike the hawks, the local sparrow population became increasingly wary of my efforts to get on close terms and would vanish from the rooftops at the instant I was spotted carrying the gun under my arm. At times I was forced to resort to the local butcher for scraps of heart, liver and lights but, as I received no monetary reward for attending school, in due course the need arose to invent other, more successful and inexpensive means of securing a regular food supply.

The most effective among a wide range of devices was a small netting trap, a somewhat primitive form of the old birdcatcher's 'back net', which could be employed with some degree of success during the night at the sparrows' roosting places. Along the back wall of the stables was a large and luxuriant growth of dark, tangled ivy, its creepers running up the timbered walls to roof level, where a few determined limbs clung to the weathered slates. The mass of ivy, its roots originating from a huge bed of stinging nettles, was a popular roost for hordes of sparrows. It was there that the trap best served its purpose. The trap itself consisted of two short ash poles about four feet in length, with a yard or so of pliable netting in between. The small mesh net, a piece of old strawberry net pinched from the garden shed, was fashioned in the form of a loose bag in which the sparrows were caught – perhaps.

When the cool of the evening descended, hordes of sparrows customary retired to the ivy clump for the night, amid much chirruping and squabbling as they fought for the more desirable perches. Having carefully noted where the majority of the birds had settled I waited for darkness to fall and then advanced to the spot with due stealth. Holding the poles apart, one in each hand, with the bag hanging loosely between them, I proceeded to beat repeatedly and somewhat erratically among the ivy, flushing out all but the most stubborn of birds from the dark mass of creepers and with any luck into the waiting net. The vast majority were lost in the inevitable confusion that followed but an unlucky few usually entangled themselves in its clinging folds to assist with the seemingly endless task of providing food.

What I really needed was larger game and I decided to try my luck at snaring rabbits. Having already discovered a well-tenanted warren at the end of old Herbert's garden I bought a dozen snares from the local hardware store for the outlay of threepence (1p) each. I didn't think the old boy would mind me snaring his garden, especially as I never told him of my plans, for, as he often remarked with a twinkle in his eye, 'It's no good getting old if you don't get artful'. So be it.

I met old Herbert on my way to lay the wires, as usual propping up his front gate and fumigating the surrounding countryside with his pipe. His gnarled features brightened visibly when he saw the bundle of snares dangling from my belt and in the text 20 minutes I received the advice of a real veteran in the art of setting rabbit snares. Catching rabbits was quite simple, Herbert explained, adding the fact that he had often caught two at once in a single wire. I took that one with a pinch of salt.

Assuring myself that I would be quite content to catch even one rabbit at a time, I left him deep in his reminiscences and walked along the lane until well out of sight before doubling back to the sheltered end of his garden. Within the hour I had finished. The dozen snares were placed with infinite and exacting care along some of the many runs or tracks leading from each inhabited burrow. Each was set at four fingers' height (required according to the gospel of old Herbert) which would – or should – ensure that the rabbits were taken cleanly. A couple were placed directly over the mouths of burrows – a complete waste of time, as any warrener will tell you – anchored by a long stake of almost fence-post proportions hammered into the sandy earth, with the running noose held in position by a small split prop or tealer.

The following evening I set out to collect my first bag of snared rabbits. Having taken a voluminous sack in which to collect the slain I was somewhat disillusioned to find the first snare still empty. I was even more disheartened to discover the remaining eleven in an identical condition, without so much as the merest trace of rabbit fur to show for my efforts. Throughout the following week I checked the snares religiously each evening, but still a capture evaded me, although on odd occasions a few wires had been knocked over or pulled into the hedge. This was certainly not good enough. Concentrating my sole efforts on one single well-used burrow, where earth and sand had been piled up to great heights from the rabbits' underground excavations, I reset the dozen wires to encircle the complete hole, the finished area resembling a World War 2 scene of an entanglement surrounding a high security prison camp. Nothing could possibly ever get out of that!

Thus I achieved my first capture. As I approached the burrow expectantly the following morning I noted with no little satisfaction that one of the wires had been pulled with some force into the nearby hedge. Parting the undergrowth I was suddenly greeted by a fierce ginger tom, snarling and spitting in an extremely agitated manner and baring a set of enormous fangs as it leapt towards me. Apparently cats – like elephants – never forget. This particular feline had been maliciously victimised in my early catapult days, often straying into our garden to hunt but instead receiving a shower of marbles to send it on its ignominious way. He at once repaid a long outstanding debt with a series of deep and painful clawmarks. Luckily for him, immediate food supplies were not at too low an ebb and I eventually released the ungrateful bundle of fur, claws and gnashing teeth, protecting myself by entangling his weaponry within the folds of the sack, which had eventually proved its worth. To help him on his way I renewed the debt between us by the swift application of a wellington boot.

Try as I might I somehow seemed incapable of catching even the smallest and most inexperienced of rabbits, although the occasional cock pheasant was captured, as was a very agitated Jack Russell terrier. The former were quite easily disposed of in the kitchen, but the latter required something of a gymnastic feat to release it without causing grievous bodily harm to it or me.

My snares were taken up for the last time when I turned my efforts towards what I thought was a far more effective means of taking rabbits, with the assistance of a huge jack ferret. Coming from a good working strain of animals he certainly possessed all the necessary tools of his trade, including an immaculate set of pearly white teeth. He was also well versed in the art of using them. Diving my hand into the stuffy interior of his travelling box, my finger was seized with a plier-like aggression normally reserved for the toughest of rabbits, enabling me to transfer him, thus suspended, to his new hutch. The most difficult job was trying to convince him that my hand was indeed not a rabbit, a fact heeded only when I had choked him off energetically with my free and comparatively unmutilated hand. He obviously needed some attention. This he subsequently received and in due course and with repeated handling the ferret became much more docile, only attempting to clamp down on a finger if my movements were sudden or unpredictable. Ferrets usually learn to recognise their handlers by sight, scent and the touch of the hand; mine preferred to be on more intimate terms, identifying his handler by taste also.

Very soon we sallied forth on the first ferreting expedition, 'we' being Ken, a former playmate and troublemaker from the adjoining village, my cousin John, a few years older than myself, who had agreed to ferry us from hole to hole in his car, me and the ferret, complete with collar and line on which to fasten the little brute when working out the burrows. In the first twenty minutes we had discovered an unusually shallow hole and bagged its single occupant, and the ferret had deposited something particularly obnoxious on the back seat of the car as we bumped along, windows now wide open, to the next venue. This was the side of a steep hill where a hedge of stunted oaks and thick blackthorn concealed a goodly number of well-used burrows.

Perhaps I should briefly explain the method of using the 'line'

ferret. The whole process is really rather simple and straightforward – theoretically, at least. Having found a suitable burrow the
ferret, with collar and line attached, is allowed to descend along
the maze of tunnels until it scents, chases and finally catches a
rabbit underground. When it has killed, the ferret will remain
with its prey until the warrener eventually finds it by excavating a
series of holes, following the path of the line as he progresses into
the uncharted depths. If digging operations are carried out with
all haste, the lucky warrener will be able to secure at least one
rabbit for each set of holes dug; but if valuable time is wasted all
he will discover at the end of the line is a very bloated ferret which
has wasted no time in reducing its catch to a collection of skin and
bones, together with the useless and smelly paunch.

Our next burrow was not as easy as the first. The ferret,
obviously hot on the heels of rabbit number two, proceeded to
take with it about 20 feet of line before finally catching up with its
quarry in the depths of the sandy hillside. A few muffled thumps
and a high pitched squeal told of a satisfactory conclusion to the
chase. All we now had to do was find them.

After two solid hours of taking turns on the single spade, we
had excavated quite a number of reasonably good-sized elephant

pits. Of the ferret there was not a sign. Almost despairing of ever setting eyes on the dear little creature again, we were suddenly surprised to see it wander out from a completely different tunnel in something approaching a bloated stupor, leaving behind a pair of meatless legs and a pile of guts as a reward for our labours. I went off ferrets, and the hawks, of necessity, went off rabbits, at least until I could devise some effective method of catching them.

My food problems seemed insoluble and one morning I found myself in a really desperate situation. On the previous day both birds had been fed on a very slender ration of fresh meat, a single house sparrow divided meticulously between the two — hardly sufficient to keep one alive and in good condition. I was out around the stables and henhouse before school with the air rifle, but with hardly a sparrow in sight, let alone in range, I began to despair of getting something to ease the food shortage. Passing the aviary I was instantly greeted by the sight of both hawks flying to the front wire of their enclosure, voicing loud and really pitiful screams as they demanded to see what I had brought for their breakfast. I had nothing.

At that very moment a herring gull passed overhead, gliding on set wings barely thirty feet above me. Almost without thinking I threw the gun to my shoulder and fired. The gull swerved evasively but after a few hasty wing-beats it continued on its original course, apparently unscathed. Oh well, at least it was worth a try. I watched it fly off with a sinking heart, but even as I turned to go the bird folded up and plummeted earthwards, pitching down apparently stone dead a hundred yards away. My prayers had been answered!

My problems, however, were only just beginning. Obviously of an uncooperative nature, the gull had somehow contrived to fall in the middle of a neighbour's garden. Either by chance or design it had chosen to drop dead within the well-guarded property of an elderly lady who was not especially fond of me or my sporting pursuits. She disliked killing, even if it was in the interest of keeping a pair of hungry hawks alive. My problem was how to retrieve the gull without incurring her wrath. I debated briefly on whether to go and ask her outright for access to her garden, but finally decided against it. What could I have said?

'Could I make a brief inspection of your orchard?' No, she

would suspect an ulterior motive immediately, especially as I had already discovered that her apple trees were now laden with delicious ripening fruit. How about, 'Please could I have my gull back?' That didn't sound right either.

I came to the conclusion that I would have to resort to stealth and cunning, and risk the chance of her seeing me from her front window which, much to my annoyance, overlooked the neatly laid out gardens and apple orchard. Working on the assumption that 'what the eye does not see . . .', I crept past the boarded front gate on all fours, hugging the ground to avoid being spotted and gaining the welcome sanctuary of a gooseberry patch that formed part of the front hedge. A white object showed plainly through a gap in the bushes. My gull, enough food for at least two days, lay stone dead about six feet from the gooseberry clump. Pulling my school cap across my face as protection from the thorns I forced myself forward into the gap, carefully enlarging it as I went. Presently my head popped out on the other side beneath rows of tall and heavily burdened apple trees. There, lying flat on its back with its pair of pink webbed paddles pointing skywards, was my hawks' breakfast, almost within reach. Stretching out at full length, my fingers were just curling around an outstretched foot when it happened. Unbeknown to me I had already been spotted. The old lady suddenly surprised me from the rear.

'Caught you at last!' she exclaimed with no little satisfaction, catching sight of my rear end protruding from the other side of the hedge. 'I thought it was you that had been pinching my gooseberries!'

How on earth she recognised me from where she stood has always remained a mystery but at length I emerged, red-faced, clutching the hard-won prize. Caught redhanded! It was no use trying to explain that a bellyful of gooseberries could not at that moment have been further from my mind. I hadn't even been near the bushes for at least two days. Already late for school and with a pair of screaming hawks still waiting to be fed, I clasped the gull to my breast and bolted.

School, however dull and claustrophobic, admittedly had its uses. During the early days I searched among the well-stocked shelves of the library, eventually securing a book on birds of prey. It clearly described the wide range of hawks and falcons, their habitats and feeding requirements, but contained only a brief chapter outlining the various hazards and pitfalls of training a hunting bird. The sport of falconry, I read, could be traced back through history for at least four thousand years, when people first trained the hawk to hunt for them and to catch their supply of meat. The sport, although no longer a necessity after the advent of the shotgun and rifle, had been carried on right up to the present day, but sadly modern exponents of the art were steadily dwindling in numbers. The kestrel, it appeared, was of little use in actual hunting, due mainly to its relatively small size and the lack of a suitable quarry at which to fly the trained bird. It could, however, be taught to fly to the fist and lure, and was considered an ideal bird for the apprentice falconer.

The first and most difficult stage of training entailed getting the hawk as tame and manageable as possible or, as it was described in the book, 'manned'. When fully manned and oblivious of the actions of man, beast and machine, the bird must then be taught to fly to the hand, or fist, for its food, thereby learning to return to the falconer at his beck and call when eventually allowed the liberty of free flight.

I would make a start immediately. After tracing an illustration from the book I cut out and fashioned a pair of jesses, or leg straps, from a strip of light, supple leather, and with much difficulty and a considerable number of deep scratches succeeded in fitting them to the largest hawk, apparently the female of the pair. I realised with regret that the task of training both birds simultaneously was beyond my powers in the limited time available. The choice had to be made of either playing truant from school for at the very least a month, or leaving the smaller male largely to his own devices. Not daring to miss out on too many maths lessons – my report invariably bore the inscription 'Could do better' – and fearing repercussions from the school inspector, I reluctantly settled for the latter alternative.

Eventually adopting me as the provider of their varied though somewhat irregular meals, both kestrels became really tame and confiding and in due course readily flew to my hand within the confines of the aviary. The male, or tiercel, displayed scant affection towards his beneficiary, seeming to look upon me as a form of animated meat wagon, but with the female I progressed a stage further, taking her out to the nearby meadow each day and flying her over increasingly long distances to my glove for food. At first a strong fishing line was attached to her jesses to foil any attempts at escape, but this was finally removed to allow the little hawk the full use of her aerial powers. After regular practice sessions she displayed all manner of skills in her flying and presently began to hunt. Her first 'kill' was a large crane fly taken on the way to the glove and, finding it well suited to her discerning palate, she keenly searched for more. The range of quarry was extended to include the huge black flying beetles found in prolific numbers among the meadow grass and over the short corn stubble in late summer. The dor beetles were taken easily in flight between her swift and accurate talons and were considered a real delicacy. They were consumed slowly and with evident relish, after each minute particle of the brittle wing casings had been carefully removed with her beak.

During those long and seemingly endless days of a scorching summer I experienced some of the happiest and most exciting times of my life. But all good things must come to an end, and one windy September afternoon, disaster struck.

I had taken the little falcon out as usual, placing her on the familiar wooden gate at the meadow entrance as I had done so many times before. There she sat bobbing her head, keen, expectant and waiting for me to call her. I walked away upwind and called her to the glove for a portion of sparrow meat. She came towards me fast, beating low over the tall flowering stems of yellow ragwort standing above the meadow grass, but instead of alighting on the offered glove she swept quickly by to climb steadily into a stiff westerly breeze. The kestrel hung momentarily overhead as the wind sang through her pinions. She circled once as if to get her bearings and then, totally ignoring my calls from far below, allowed herself to be swept away over a nearby belt of yellowing oaks. I ran after her in growing desperation, but several minutes had elapsed before I finally reached the trees. On the far side of the copse only a confused squadron of lapwings wheeled and dived skilfully amongst themselves in an otherwise empty sky. Further away in the distance a dark shape detached itself from the dead branch of a prominent oak on the horizon, but my hopes plummeted as I recognised the familiar sneaking outline of a carrion crow.

I had already seen the last of my hawk, for although I searched in mounting despair until darkness called a halt that day, and for many days afterwards, not a trace was ever found of the bird I had grown to look upon with great affection. For many days I was overcome with a terrible sense of loss, only then fully appreciating how deeply involved I had become with my first hawk. I consoled myself with the fact that she had at least learned how to hunt and catch large insects, and with luck on her side should be able to fend for herself until the colder winter months. By that time, if she survived, it was quite possible that she would have learned the ways of taking and killing more substantial prey, thus ensuring her future survival in the countryside of her wild ancestors.

The sadly limited spell with the bird had not only provided me with many happy hours and memories, it had also stirred some age-old dormant instinct and excitement within me, laying a firm foundation for the years that were to follow. However, the tiercel was kept in the aviary until he died several years later, as I could not bring myself to train him after losing the female kestrel. One day, I promised myself, I would own a real hunting bird, with which I would pursue and catch the wild game of the countryside.

3

Of Things That Go Bump

My painful introduction to the unknown powers of the shotgun was one experience which at the time I would gladly have drawn a veil over, but now the bruise on my shoulder has long gone and the equally painful blow to my pride healed, perhaps the incident is worth the mention.

It happened one chilly November afternoon, a day of watery skies and a cutting wind which sent flurries of tinted leaves swirling to the ground, where squirrels and jays hunted among the leaf litter for the harvest of fallen acorns. During the afternoon I had been lending a hand on the farm, carting a few loads of sugar beet tops to feed the farm cattle. Cousin John, he who had driven the car on the ferreting expedition, was in need of a pheasant or two, and as we prepared to collect the last load of cattle fodder late in the afternoon he stopped at the farmhouse to collect his gun, an old box-lock ejector bought just after the war and made by British Small Arms.

We bumped and rattled along the deserted country lane, John at the wheel of the tractor and myself perched rather precariously on the trailer draw-bar, enviously nursing his twelve-bore and repeatedly downing imaginary cock pheasants all along our route. As we rattled past a hillside cattle enclosure John pointed out a real cock pheasant, strutting large as life in full view and no more than forty yards from the roadside. Then to my sheer delight he skidded to a halt, handed me a couple of cartridges and at the same time indicated towards the bird. Filled with apprehension I obeyed, my hands shaking uncontrollably as I slipped the cartridges into the breech. Quietly clicking the gun shut I alighted from the trailer draw-bar and crept stealthily forward, keeping my head well below the bank vegetation to avoid detection, and at last reached a comfortable position about 35 yards from where the old bird stood quietly preening. Slipping the safety catch forward, I raised the mighty weapon to my shoulder and prepared to fire. The beautiful old cock, which no doubt owed his longevity to some mysterious sixth sense, suddenly became aware that something was amiss and raised an inquisitive head in the air to scan his surroundings, before deciding on what course of evasive action the situation demanded. Remaining in a kneeling posture I drew a positive bead along the seemingly enormous barrels and then slowly eased back the trigger.

That was the last I saw of the pheasant. Being of small stature the resulting 'Whooomph!' sent me sprawling backwards, my ears singing with the unaccustomed and deafening explosion and my right shoulder throbbing painfully with the mule-like kick of the recoil. When I eventually plucked up courage to open my eyes there was no sign of the pheasant or, for that matter, of the field it had been standing in. All I saw was a patch of open sky. The gun had knocked me flat! Unlike Herbert, who would undoubtedly have had a hidden and well-padded rabbit to cushion his fall, my rear end had come firmly into contact with the hard granite surface of the road.

John jumped off the tractor and struggled to assist me to a more dignified vertical posture, struggling even harder to suppress his amusement at my plight. Of the pheasant there was not a sign. He had departed hotfoot to pastures new, leaving not so much as a feather behind him to mark the spot where a veritable

cloud of number six shot had sped through the air on a fruitless mission, cutting a wide and unsightly swathe through the lush pasture grass.

However, pride and honour were soon restored. As we resumed our journey past the adjoining field I saw a single hen pheasant, obviously wary of the nearby explosion as it squatted low amongst a patch of tall barley stubble. It rose at a distance of at least 40 yards as I crept towards it, not even allowing me the advantage of a sitting shot. Almost without thinking I threw the gun to my shoulder, firing at the instant the stock connected. The result was two-fold: the charge knocked the pheasant from the sky and blew me from my feet. Luckily I was the first to recover and my first flying pheasant was soon safely in the bag.

Unbeknown to my parents, who quite rightly considered it unwise for such a small boy to roam the countryside with a potentially lethal firearm, I often sneaked off to the farm to borrow John's gun, taking my air rifle to account for my success if I was lucky enough to return home with a dinner. With much practice I eventually mastered the technique of remaining upright against the mule-like recoil and my standard of shooting improved accordingly. My parents became suspicious only when discovering a telltale pattern of shot in plucked game instead of the usual single pellet of an air rifle. This led to the temporary curtailment of my shooting activities, but I eventually managed to persuade father to accompany me on a few occasions until I was at last considered reliable and safe enough to be allowed to shoot alone. I became the very model of safety, except for one small lapse when I almost succeeded in blowing the toes off my right foot while carrying the gun fully cocked beneath my arm. Luckily for a new pair of wellingtons, the charge missed by an inch. Equally lucky, it taught me a lesson for life; to treat the business end of a shotgun with all due respect.

This lesson was further emphasised on my first appearance among the team of guns at the annual hare shoot, one of those delightfully informal but notoriously dangerous occasions held in the hope of reducing the hare population to a more accommodating level, thereby preventing excess damage to growing corn and root crops in the spring. On such missions the guns are divided into standing and walking groups. The walkers drive the hares forward, as they are disturbed from their forms on the open fields, towards the line of guns spaced at regular intervals at the end of each beat, where, according to the guns' standard of marksmanship, the hares are met with well-placed shots or well-chosen oaths. In theory nothing could be safer. In truth it is quite the reverse. The main snag lies in the fact that large numbers of guns are required to cover wide areas of open ground adequately, and it is difficult to amass the large number of marksmen required without enlisting the services of one or two dubious individuals who, to put it bluntly, hardly know the muzzle from the breech.

When the two lines converge with the hares between them it would often seem advantageous to be wearing a bulletproof vest or to seek a position where one could prepare to drop flat in the nearest furrow.

On the day in question there was one such person whom, to save embarrassment, I shall refer to as Charlie. Charlie, despite his 70-odd years, had remained as keen as mustard when a gun was placed in his rather unsteady hand, and he normally carried a rusty and pitted smokepole which had also seen far better days. The first two drives went off without so much as a stray pellet and by mid-morning we had accumulated a fair number of hares, besides half a dozen rabbits and the odd pigeon or two for good measure. The third drive, a seemingly endless area of sticky plough, was to be the last before the lunchbreak. At the end of the field several hares were accounted for as they attempted to cross the line of guns placed in strategic positions along the otherwise deserted country lane.

After the pick-up Charlie, draped in a black waterproof mackintosh of almost tentlike proportions, strolled over to where we, the standing guns, had formed a small circle to discuss the events of the morning's sport.

'Knocked up yet, Charlie?' one of the guns enquired with a sly grin, knowing that he had been taking it easy while the walkers plodded on through acres of sticky mud.

'I'm not done for yet', Charlie replied, attempting to knock about three stone of clinging mud from each wellington boot and gazing with a certain relief at the expanse of treacle-like substance over which he had somehow managed to navigate from the far horizon. Turning back to face us, he took the old hammer gun from beneath his arm, in the process catching a fully cocked hammer within the folds of his coat. A scorching flame lanced from the muzzle and our eardrums were shattered by a deafening explosion.

Rooted to the spot and unable to appreciate our near escape, we gazed as one in awe at a huge gaping hole that had suddenly appeared inside the small circle made by our feet, from which a faint wisp of smoke curled ominously upwards. It was impossible to determine who was the more surprised or frightened, Charlie or we, but I did notice that all faces, formerly jovial, had turned a deathly white.

'I . . . I . . . I was just about to unload it', Charlie stammered, obviously deeply ashamed and shocked by the thought of what might have happened.

'You've just saved yourself the trouble', retorted one of the guns. Further comment would have been superfluous. Charlie walked alone in the afternoon.

The seasons came and went, seasons during which I spent most of my spare time carrying the gun under my arm, walking the fields, woods and marshes to my heart's content and learning all the time to take pleasure in the endless sights, sounds and scents that nature unveiled with the turning of the year. It was all too good to last.

At the age of sixteen, when I first heard the news that we were to move house, I was quite excited at the prospect of indulging in some of the luxuries we had been denied for so long. Electricity, television, water from a tap — all conspired to make me forget the freedom which I would leave behind. When the time came to leave the roof that had sheltered me for so many of my young years, I at last knew how terrible homesickness could be, spending the first few days in our new home in a state of semi-conscious shock. Gone was the view from my bedroom window across the open fields, where flocks of green plover tumbled and tossed to their hearts' content; their plaintive wailings were replaced by the shrieks and screams of Homo sapiens. Gone were the green and leafy hedgerows, so full of adventure and teeming with untold secrets waiting to be discovered. Lost too was the sparkling river, whose unseen depths concealed all manner of thrills for a country boy who revelled in a world of his own. The new village, however small by today's standards, was in my eyes dull and claustrophobic, inhabited by countless humans in place of the wild people I had come to know as denizens of marsh, wood, riverside and country lane. No longer could I wander with catapult or gun literally out of the back door into the deserted fields to become as one with the trees, flowers and wildlife that I had regarded as eternal. We had moved only a few miles to the village but I somehow felt cut off from my former everyday life, even though I returned whenever I could to regain a few hours of freedom.

Sport was hard to come by and excitements few and far between, though gradually I began to kindle an interest in what sport was available in the village, indulging when the opportunity allowed in a return to my former way of life. I made good friends. One of these was Ken, my ferreting companion and former playmate, who had made an identical move to the same village a few years earlier. He had also retained an interest in the outdoor life and together we shared many an adventure.

Ken and I were standing by the road bridge one evening, as usual discussing solutions to the problem of the acute shortage of female companions, when Ken suddenly pointed to a spot a hundred yards further along the road where a stand of tall alder trees created a natural tunnel over the road. There, resplendent in his chain mail plumage, an old cock pheasant stood, the brilliance of his feathers glinting warmly in the last rays of the dying sun.

'At least there's one bird that's not in short supply', commented Ken drily, as the huge old pheasant strutted boldly across the road, proud as a peacock, before fluttering noisily to the lower branches of an ivy-draped alder overhanging a small backwater where he was to spend the night. This was rather more than we could take. We both agreed that a bird in the hand was worth at least two in the alder bush and with this in mind planned to return later with my air rifle under the cover of darkness.

Three hours later we were back, both equally apprehensive under the glaring light of a full December moon. The old gentleman was easily located, sitting hunched on a slender bough and dark against the brightness of the sky, his feathers fluffed out to hold sufficient warmth to keep the rigours of a sharp frost at bay. But alas, he was not so easily to be brought to hand, for as we crept towards him through the crisp undergrowth a twig cracked sharply underfoot and he was gone, a mere fleeting shadow and a sound of whirring wings as he receded into the dark distance. Our bird had flown. Filled with disappointment we began the journey home.

It was then that we had a rather narrow escape. In our concentration on the pheasant we had completely forgotten about the local gamekeeper, who habitually travelled the same stretch of road each night to sink a pint or two of beer at his favourite local. He was almost upon us before we heard the clanking of his ancient bicycle. Surely we were caught? Walking along the middle of the road with the gun under my arm, there was no time to bolt for cover and absolutely no chance of remaining undetected in the bright moonlight. Then Ken, normally a rational character, suddenly did a strange thing. He threw his arms around me in what must have looked akin to a fit of tender passion, hiding the incriminating – and mercifully unloaded – gun between us out of sight. With a friendly 'Goodnight' the keeper clanked by, seeing only two lovers out for a romantic stroll in the bright moonlight. I almost felt him blush with embarrassment as he passed us by.

Fishing provided another welcome outlet for our enthusiasm. The River Wensum flowed along the eastern end of the village, passing beneath a bridge beside a picturesque old paper mill. The bridge was an ideal vantage point from which to scan the waters below for its piscatorial inhabitants. Another regular visitor to the bridge was the local water bailiff, whose job it was to keep a careful eye on the local inhabitants, both finned and two-legged, and occasionally to attempt to check our nonexistent fishing licences. Actually we were not unduly bothered, for he was rather a small man and was normally suffering the consequences of an overdose of Scotch whisky. Nevertheless, however inebriated, he had the backing of the area river authority, so it was in our best interests to keep on the right side of him.

Early one summer, the river board decided to restock what they considered were some of the suitable stretches of the River

Wensum with large quantities of hand-reared trout. The bridges were one of the areas chosen as a release point. One morning a team of workmen arrived to net the area downstream of the waterfall in an attempt to clear some of the less desirable predatory fish from the water, to give the newly introduced trout the chance of a better start in their new environment. An electric shock wave was set off and passed through the water, stunning any fish that swam within its range. Many floated almost lifeless to the surface and were carried in a dazed condition by the swift current, to be netted by a line of men waiting in the gravelly shallows further downstream. A surprising number of pike, perch and eels were taken by the nets, leaving many of the harmless roach, dace and lesser fry to recover when the effects of the shock wore off.

A few days later tanks containing several hundred trout of varying sizes arrived at the bridge and were released in the demilitarised zone, for the present safe from attack by predatory species. But they were not safe for long. The board had not reckoned on the local force of human predators, which now skulked in the background like a pack of vultures over a fresh kill. Almost as soon as the dust had settled behind the departing lorries, fishing rods miraculously appeared as if from thin air and a veritable barrage of worms, bread paste and maggots hit the water. Having been used to hand feeding, in no time at all a large number of gleaming trout lay flapping and gasping on the grassy banks. The board had not chosen their release site with much deliberation, and a large percentage of their charges were quickly transferred from basking under the bridge in the sun to basking rather more deliciously under a hot grill.

Unlicensed trout fishing became such a popular pastime in the locality that the bailiff's visits became all too frequent, so intent did he become on discovering the cause of the trout's quite alarming and unprecedented decrease in numbers. It became necessary for us to devise less conspicuous methods of ensuring grilled trout was not a rarity on the dinner table. I discarded my rod, instead utilising a simple wooden reel and line which could be quickly wound up and concealed in a pocket if the bailiff should suddenly appear. But despite taking precautions, one afternoon I was caught redhanded.

I was fishing from the bridge, clinging rather precariously between the steel safety girders lining the edge of the road and dunking a bunch of small red worms into two feet of crystal water. I had already hauled out a nice plump fish of a pound and a quarter which was safely in my pocket, but another of at least two pounds had taken over the recently vacated lie to tempt me from the shallows, its tail fanning gently to hold position in the current behind a slimy silkweed-covered boulder. Once having gained experience, trout are highly selective feeders. Time and time again the bunch of wriggling worms drifted past it, on occasion almost brushing along its silver flanks, but, although darting from side to side to snap up morsels of more natural food carried to it by the flow, the fish stubbornly refused my offer of an easy meal. Quite a rogue's gallery had gathered to watch the proceedings, continually proffering words of advice and eagerly awaiting the moment when the trout could resist no more.

During the excitement a large van drew up on the narrow parking area 30 yards away and from it stepped a family of strangers we had not seen before. As the bridge and its waterfall are considered a local beauty spot it was not unusual for visitors to stop nearby and stroll along the quiet road, taking in the scene and trying to spot shoals of silver fish twisting and darting in the clear water. The new arrivals attracted little more than a cursory glance. They were a typical family outing – or so we were led to believe. After first inspecting the far side of the bridge the group strolled casually over towards us, apparently taking not the slightest interest in what we were about. It was all too casual somehow. I tried to relax and half-heartedly resumed fishing, but only for a few minutes.

'Were we', the head of the family enquired with forced politeness, 'ever troubled by the water bailiff?'

At the very mention of the most honourable gentleman's name I felt my stomach churn and my knees turn to jelly. Something was definitely amiss!

'Oh', retorted one of our crowd, not renowned for his superfluous wit, 'if the bailiff troubles us, we'll sling him in the river!'

There was a definite and meaningful silence, after which the stranger, rather less politely, informed us that he was indeed the bailiff and, to boot, he had no intention of ending up in the river. The board had matched our underhand methods by changing the patrol man on our stretch of river. Unlike his predecessor, this particular gentleman was all of six feet two, extremely well built and decidedly sober. By the time I had recovered my wits a heated argument had started up and the bailiff appeared to have lost interest in me for the moment, so in the confusion that followed, as the group discussed the merits of the water board and trout fishing licences and theoretically and repeatedly slung each other in the river, I made the most of the opportunity to make myself scarce, quietly melting into an adjoining copse and gaining welcome sanctuary in the hedges and fields that had become as familiar as the back of my hand.

Much of our fishing thereafter was carried out during the hours of darkness. For three of us each Saturday night was reserved for a regular all-night eeling session. There was little evidence of eels during the daylight hours and few were caught then, but at nightfall the eels emerged from holes and crannies and from under rocks in the crumbling bridge foundations to feed in earnest, snapping up any tasty morsels brought down-stream by the water's flow. On Saturday nights they would encounter a profusion of unaccustomed delicacies – squashed gudgeon, dead herrings and sprats, bundles of worms and any well-matured lump of fish or meat, the smellier and ghastlier the better. Those that succumbed to temptation were hauled bodily up the side of the bridge, usually causing a few minutes of panic and confusion. The trouble was that the eels often came on to feed simultaneously. We would sit for hours on end with not so much as a nibble or the quiver of a rod tip, but suddenly, as if to a prearranged signal, the river would appear to boil with hooked fish. Standing on a narrow ledge above the foaming river with a rod apiece, the three of us would all attempt to bank an eel at the same time, causing utter pandemonium as our lines crossed and recrossed, often ending up with an invisible bird's nest of nylon and a trio of lost eels.

Occasionally our luck held, but it still required considerable gymnastic abilities to bring our catch to hand. Coated with a thick slime of cart-grease consistency, eels are almost as adept at moving about on land as they are in water, as we soon found out to our cost. All three of us banked an eel simultaneously on one occasion, and the ensuing pursuit in almost total darkness was akin to a midnight snake hunt. It was some time and several lost eels later that we learned the trick of dropping them on an open newspaper, which absorbed the slime and caused instant immobility, far preferable to having a large eel giving a slimy imitation of a greased anaconda around one's arm.

Our Saturday night eeling sessions proved extremely popular. Very soon others were keen to join us. In most cases parents were the main obstacle, as few were willing to allow their offspring the thrill of discovering the delights of spending a cold night on an exposed bridge above several feet of even colder water, and in due course we were called upon to assist in various manoeuvres to enable others to join us.

One particular family of two boys and a girl were blessed with very strict parents who, we were informed, were very light sleepers. How could the three get out? To a prearranged plan we arrived beneath their bedroom window at a few minutes past midnight, one of our number – who could supply almost anything on request – humping a 30-foot stack ladder on his back along the main street. A handful of shingle on the window pane announced our arrival. A shorter ladder would have helped matters greatly, but we eventually managed to position the monstrosity against the window ledge at an angle of 45 degrees, mercifully missing the overhead power cables but effectively blocking the road, with its base propped several yards away in the adjacent field. The rest was easy. A later repeat of the operation, however, was not.

The ladder had been moved to another site on the farm for more orthodox use, forcing us to resort to a wagon rope for the assisted escape. With instructions to fasten it to something solid, the rope was flicked up through the open window and quickly secured. The girl, though never having climbed a rope before, was the bravest of the reluctant trio. Alas, she was also the heaviest. With a clatter like a pair of skeletons making love on a hot tin roof she descended at an unwarranted speed to join us 20 feet below, giving her parents' bedroom window a hefty kick on the way down for good measure. The three's idea of something solid had been the bed, to one leg of which the rope had been secured. Positioned on the far wall at the opposite end of the bedroom, it had grated noisily across the floorboards as the girl descended and almost followed the truants out of the window. We waited, holding our breaths, for their parents to come and see what was going on – but not a sound came from the house apart from a gentle rhythmic snoring from the bottom bedroom. So much for the light sleepers!

In fact, we were never discovered, and we spent many an enthralling night on the bridge in pursuit of the eel, scrumping apples and enjoying a number of midnight barbecues, until I eventually passed my driving test at the third attempt, allowing me to travel back and forth to my old hunting grounds with ease.

At about this time a gravel company had begun excavations on one of the larger meadows, having discovered large areas of sand and gravel beneath the virtually useless – from a farming point of view – sedge and reed beds, interspersed with deep and often quite dangerous drainage channels. Little did I realise what a vast transformation was about to take place. The huge diggers and draglines were busy for long hours, scarring and gouging wide tracts of virgin marshland where once the ragged robin, the water forget-me-not and the golden flag lilies lined the spongy drain banks, and the crafty marsh pheasant skulked among the yellowing sedge beds.

After a few months a broad lake began to form in the wake of the retreating draglines. A number of gravelly islands were left dotted about in strategic positions, tastefully relieving the monotony of such a vast sheet of water and providing shelter and nesting cover for the wide variety of new life that the water attracted. Besides the challenge of the cock pheasant and the grating 'churr' of the reed warbler, the lake now echoed with the thrilling calls of wildfowl, mallard, teal, tufted duck and pochard, and the musical orchestrations of literally scores of Canada geese. There was an obvious sporting potential. Many of the wildfowl moved at dawn and dusk between the lake and a similar refuge two miles distant. The highlights of these moves were the magnificent flights of geese in great wedge-shaped formations a hundred or more strong, their bugling cries echoing musically throughout the entire length of the river valley.

Eventually the geese, despite their indisputable enhancement of the valley, increased in such numbers as to become a menace, grazing and spoiling large areas of lush grazing intended for cattle and attacking fields of young corn like a squadron of winged lawn mowers. It was high time to reduce the massed ranks to a more convenient level. Several birds fell to my gun but the geese grew rapidly warier, remaining much higher during dawn and dusk flights and only lessening height and speed when over the safety of water. What I really needed was a boat.

My experience with boats was sadly lacking, to say the least. I finally reached the decision that the ideal craft would be something along the lines of the old-fashioned coastal wildfowler's punt; about 20 feet long, flat and inconspicuous on water and virtually impossible to sink or turn over – the last requirement being of prime importance. So much for ideals. Not being particularly well off at the time and noting with horror the exorbitant price of such a craft, I settled for a considerably smaller inflatable job, purchased through a mail order firm. In due course the boat, or what passed for it, arrived through the post in an incredibly small package, complete with foot pump, air connection tube and full inflating instructions. The oars, I was assured, would arrive soon after, the company being out of stock at the present time.

It soon became apparent that the rubber 'all purpose' dinghy was not all it was cracked up to be. The most immediately obvious feature was that instead of being a nice neutral colour to blend in happily with its surroundings, the thing was a brilliant shade of orange – not the easiest of colours to make inconspicuous among the greys, greens and browns of its intended home. The next disappointment was the 'high speed foot pump', a weird and flimsy contraption resembling a half-inflated Christmas balloon, complete with a length of what seemed like valve rubber to be used as a connecting tube when inflation was in progress. Having already planned a goose foray for dawn the next morning, I set about pumping the thing up to take it to the marsh in readiness for the morning flight.

After an hour and a half of fierce pumping that made me weak at the knees, the boat began to assume the appearance of an oversized car tube. I dreaded to think just how long it would have taken had I plumped for the alternative 'slow speed foot pump', but at the rate I was going the oars would have arrived in time for the initial launching. When it had almost assumed correct proportions I made the mistake of expecting it to be fitted with a self-closing valve. Disconnecting the rubber tube, I lost at least twenty minutes of air in five seconds flat, before I could insert the attached bung in its rightful position. Half an hour later, it was ready.

At ten o'clock in the evening I carried it down to the river in the moonlight, the plan being to allow the current to carry me the two miles downstream to our nearest marsh. I looked forward with some trepidation to testing its waterproof qualities over 20 feet of icy water. In fact it was extremely buoyant, riding high on the surface and being carried easily by the swift current of the upper reaches. Away from the shallows the journey downstream was at a more leisurely pace, lit by the huge cheese of a moon and enhanced by a wide and exciting variety of nocturnal noises: the splash of a coypu breaking the mirrored surface, the gnawing of countless water voles and shrews and the clucking of moorhen, constantly bickering amongst themselves as they fought for an opponent's roosting perch among the darkness of the overhanging willows. High overhead, two ghost-like herons circled the moon like a pair of gigantic moths, voicing a harsh challenge that echoed through the adjacent fir woods, following the trail of the strange noctural creature that had invaded their nightly fishing grounds.

All too soon I arrived at the marsh. Tying the boat to a willow overhanging the shallows, I left the herons to their fishing and went for a few hours sleep before my dawn expedition.

Returning in the early hours of darkness I was surprised to find that a thick fog had descended during the night, cloaking all in its path and obliterating even the river banks as I untied and set off to travel downstream once again. There was still at least a mile to cover along a twisting way, where in places sunken tree trunks created a hazardous obstacle course in the murky gloom. My impulse was to hurry when I started hearing the honking of awakening geese, splashing and preening in readiness for the morning flight, but progress was restricted by the maze of fallen boughs in the water, all seeming to reach out for me as I tried to steer clear of a puncture, ears constantly attuned for the first hiss of escaping air. Several small parties of mallard and teal swished past me from time to time in the half-light of dawn, faint shadows in the gloom following the silver path of the river, and once I caught the faraway 'tok, tok' of a small flight of shoveler moving unseen along the valley.

At last I arrived at the marsh – mercifully with the boat still fully inflated – and dragged the dinghy across ten yards of boggy rush beds to the lake, lying adjacent to the path of the river. Climbing aboard once more complete with gun, cartridges and a stout branch picked up en route to use as a setting pole, I shoved off from the bank, almost immediately losing all sense of direction in the enveloping mist but enticed by the ever-increasing clamour of the geese awaiting a clear patch in the fog to enable them to move. Coot and dabchick skittered across the pewter surface of the lake before me, only to be quickly swallowed in the murky depths; and once I was startled by the snake-like head of a fishing cormorant that surfaced momentarily beside me, but was as quickly gone into the steely depths to resume its hunting.

For fully half an hour I followed the trail of goose noises at a steady crawl, their music at times sounding so close that every second I expected to see the rearguard of the massed ranks loom out of the swirling mist before me. But always the geese managed to remain one paddle ahead of me. I saw not a feather.

Nearly despairing of ever getting on terms with the geese or seeing dry land again, I suddenly detected a distinct change in their voices, a tone of urgency heralding their readiness to take to the air. The noise reached an almost deafening crescendo as hordes of geese erupted all around me, and I was suddenly rewarded by the sight of a huge squadron heading directly towards the boat and rapidly gaining height and speed. At the double report two massive shapes folded up and detached themselves from the centre of the bunch, plunging directly towards me – one with each barrel: a left and right! The following moments, however, were not ones of jubilation. A left and right at Canadas from such a vulnerable position was something along the lines of being bombed by a brace of depth charges. Two twelve-pound Canadas plummeted in the direction of the little craft, the first drenching me with icy spray and the next missing the boat behind me by a matter of inches. Having once been knocked to the ground and badly winded by a shot pigeon weighing just over a pound, I realised that a twelve-pound goose falling to join one in such a frail craft would be no laughing matter — even taking into account that one would be saving time by not having to collect it.

A few days later the set of paddles arrived, allowing me to propel the craft in a much more competent manner instead of haphazardly splashing around in dizzy circles like a whirligig beetle, putting all fowl within a quarter of a mile to flight before gaining a suitable distance. Thereafter I enjoyed many outings in the boat, at morning and evening flight and beneath the magic light of a full moon; an always exciting but equally hazardous venture in view of the many hidden obstacles lying submerged in the lake's shallower regions. Fate guided me safely for a while, but I was not to retain the services of the boat for long. At six o'clock one dark and freezing December morning I shoved out onto the lake with high hopes of a goose at morning flight. I had paddled silently to a favourite position almost in the centre of the lake in the darkness when I suddenly noticed that I appeared to be sitting rather low in the water. A faint hiss emanated from somewhere along the starboard side. Fresh out of a warm bed, the truth was slow to dawn on me. I was losing air — the boat had a puncture!

Had the occasion been during the hot days of midsummer there would have been little cause for concern, but as it was the lake was edged with a coating of glassy ice and I was encumbered with gun, thick shooting coat, two pocketfuls of cartridges and wellington boots. There was an obvious urgency to reach dry land quickly. I had to choose between the rather temporary and doubtful safety of a small island near at hand, in which case I would be hopelessly marooned until someone eventually dis-covered my plight, or making a desperate attempt to reach the sanctuary of the bank, which at that particular moment seemed an exceedingly long way off. As I was floating — for the moment — over the top of at least four fathoms of icy water, the decision, although not easy, had to be taken with all speed.

In an adventurous mood I plumbed for the latter course and, my arms flailing like the legs of a water boatman, began to propel myself and the wretched craft across the water. Progress seemed sickeningly slow as the boat, formerly easy to row across the surface but now suffering from an acute lack of air and a considerable intake of water, had taken on the appearance and manoeuvrability of a wet sack. Anyone who has attempted to steer a deflated dinghy will appreciate the problem. Round and round I went in dizzy circles, catching several crabs in the process, getting neither nearer to nor further from the desired bank but growing increasingly worried with the passing of each second. At last I devised a method of steering and after a frenzied and strenuous performance, coupled with a stroke rate that would have put many an Oxford Blue to shame, the lake-side slowly loomed larger out of the morning mist. Never before had it seemed such a welcome sight.

With a final effort from me and something resembling a watery belch from the so-called safety tanks along the dinghy's interior, the craft collapsed like a deflated balloon in the gravelly shallows. I lay like an overheated hippo for a few moments to regain my breath. Almost immediately goose voices sounded nearby — the morning flight. I turned my head to watch a huge skein of geese beat purposefully across the lake, destined for their feeding grounds further up the valley. Needless to say, the centre of the wide vee of birds passed directly over the spot I had so recently

and prematurely vacated. My comments regarding inflatable boats, morning flights and Canada geese were definitely unsuitable for reading material.

4

Have Decoys – Will Travel

My first attempts at decoying were at the request of Sam the egg producer, who begged assistance in destroying some of a particularly active strain of egg thieves that were daily relieving his henhouses of vast numbers of new-laid eggs.

My ex-playmate and now accomplice Ken, employed by Sam in his spare time cleaning eggs, led me to one of the wooden poultry houses where the most serious of a long spell of felonies had been committed. Setting two clean white eggs in a prominent spot well in range of an open window, we retired to make ourselves as comfortable as possible on the slatted floor among a number of disgruntled broody hens, the odd chicken flea and a veritable army of red mite. Mercifully there was not long to wait. A few minutes later our combined scratchings were interrupted as a single magpie came chattering hoarsely along the hedge from the tree-clad hillside opposite. Spotting the open 'nest' it swooped to avail itself of the hen's generosity. We had it for sure! But it was not to be.

Magpies, in common with the rest of their crafty cousins that form the *Corvidae* tribe, are quite rightly renowned for their exceedingly good eyesight. This particular character was no exception. Almost as soon as it touched down with beak poised beside the eggs it spotted two heads, four eyes and a pair of twelve-bore barrels framed threateningly in the henhouse window. Dispensing with a closer inspection the magpie beat a hasty retreat towards the safety of the nearest wood, chattering nineteen to the dozen and jinking from side to side with the agility of a flushed snipe. Taken by surprise I swung the gun wildly in its direction, in my haste clouting the window frame with the barrels. Three things happened in rapid succession. A very scared but otherwise unscathed magpie swerved evasively, my finger struck both triggers simultaneously and a veritable cloud of featherpecked Rhode Island Reds erupted from a nearby nettle bed, flapping and clucking disapprovingly, having been on the receiving end of the complete contents of both barrels. Luckily there were no serious casualties, but there was little point in remaining. The magpie would not return that day and I rather suspected the hens would not either. But before leaving I promised to return, first allowing the magpies a day or two to settle down before the next attempt.

The next outing was far more successful. At the end of it we ceremoniously laid six dead magpies in the egg-house and received the magnificent sum of half a crown (12.5p) from a very satisfied customer. The biggest reward, however, came from the pleasure and satisfaction of a job well done. There was also something quite fascinating about the decoying game, but as decoying magpies had obvious limitations I set about finding something that would provide more regular sport.

Wood pigeon were the obvious answer. Local farmers were plagued continually by massive and seemingly unlimited flocks of greedy birds, whose sole object in life seemed to be an all-out war on growing crops, which they pillaged, knocked down and destroyed like a vast army of miniature aerial combine harvesters. I was further encouraged by unearthing an old wooden pigeon decoy from beneath a pile of farming tools and corn sacks in the barn. It was a rather crude home-made effort, worm-eaten and faded almost beyond recognition, but when cleaned up and given a new coat of paint it looked at least reasonably lifelike at a distance. Admittedly one glass eye was missing and the grossly oversized beak tilted upwards almost at right angles, as if it had at some time flown slap into a brick wall or was possibly a member of an elite avian upper class; but the way I looked at it, if a pigeon ever got close enough to make such a detailed examination there was very little to be said for my standard of shooting.

The very next morning, armed with the decoy and father's double-barrelled twelve-bore, I set off with high hopes and a pocketful of cartridges to a freshly drilled corn field. The decoy duly took its place, propped up quite realistically on a wooden peg while I retired to await events from the concealment of a low thicket of hazel fans, keeping well in range of my wooden friend. For almost two hours I lay in wait, hardly daring to move my eyes from the decoy lest a pigeon should arrive unnoticed. This became rather boring after a while and I was about to call it a day when a solitary woodie came floating high overhead with the wind in its tail, apparently destined for the next county. It spotted the decoy and much to my astonishment dropped like a stone to join it for lunch. I knocked it down as it hovered in deep thought above my geriatric Judas, obviously unable to believe that such a decrepit looking creature could manage to survive. From that first shot I was hooked. Although no more pigeon returned then to confirm my abilities I was determined to learn more of the sport and to become proficient in the job of crop protection, which had an obviously good sporting potential.

Before I could get down to the serious business of decoying pigeon I obviously needed decoys. My loner was insignificant when set on its own in a large field, where it was generally lost from view among growing crops. What I really needed was a small flock to create a good picture of birds busily feeding on a desirable site. Being a gregarious lot, wood pigeon rarely feed alone, and it is for this reason that they cause so much damage, congregating en masse to pillage and destroy large areas of farm produce. It is also this fact that enables the experienced decoyer to amass large bags by setting out an assembly of decoys on a known and well-used feeding ground, where they will be joined quite readily by birds arriving at mealtimes.

Luckily, Santa Claus obliged by filling my Christmas stocking with a small flock of rubber decoys. I handled them with mounting excitement as I anticipated the mass exterminations that would surely follow. I could hardly wait to try them out.

Alas, my first bags were well below expectations. In fact, my initial outing produced the grand total of three birds, and even these were shot while they were passing high over the decoys without showing the slightest inclination to join them for a meal. Something was up – the pigeons, to be exact. Moreover, they remained up, for despite my repeatedly altering the shape and location of my decoying patterns, very few displayed even the remotest interest. They normally passed by at least two gunshots wide, at times shying away from my most cunningly contrived displays and inevitably drifting to alight and gorge themselves at the far end of the field I was supposed to be protecting.

It was only after a great deal of trial and error that I eventually discovered that the actual setting up of the decoys mattered much less than the area in which they were placed. I had learned a most important lesson, and the exact location of feeding flocks and the routes or flightlines by which they arrived to swell the ranks were in future noted carefully each time I arrived at the shooting area. The birds were then put to flight and replaced by my small flock. Thus when they eventually returned in ones and twos to commence feeding, the overall picture had changed little and a great many swooped without hesitation to join their rubber cousins. My efficiency as a vermin destroyer increased accordingly. Now, instead of popping off a mere handful of birds as they hesitated on the fringe of the decoy pattern, I began numbering my bags in tens, scores and eventually hundreds, propping shot birds (the best decoy of all) on wires among the decoy layout to produce a very enticing patch of blue that prompted almost every pigeon within reasonable range to investigate more closely.

Placing shot birds on ground devoid of cover worked extreme-ly well, but among growing crops it had obvious shortcomings. As the majority of my shooting took place over peas, clover, rape, lucerne and other concealing foliage, the decoys were often lost from sight to flighting birds from more than a few yards' distance, much to the detriment of the day's shooting. Experiments commenced on constructing a gadget to elevate decoys above crop level. I finally hit on the idea of bending a single strand of fencing wire into an oval, slightly less in length than a pigeon's body, to which was added a pair of stout wire legs to support the bird at heights of up to 18 inches above ground level. The supporting legs could be pushed into the ground until the desired elevation was achieved. It was but an easy matter to add another twist of wire to the front end to support the head in a lifelike position.

All this, no matter how simple it sounds, took me quite some time to work out, but I realised I had achieved something approaching perfection when a particularly amorous pigeon attempted to mate with a shot bird propped on one of my 'cradles' above a foot and a half of flowering peas. As the pair rocked and swayed precariously on the cradle, the newcomer apparently ignoring the blasé and uncooperative nature of his partner, I fired a long range shot at his rear end, which happened to be pointing in my direction. For some inexplicable reason I am consistently unreliable at sitting shots. This was no exception. At the report a cloud of feathers spouted from the decoy below. The avian Casanova, evidently puzzled by his partner's suddenly rather hot reception of his advances, spiralled high in the air and, after taking a last cautious circuit of the cradled bird, beat a hasty retreat to the nearest wood. Feeding was obviously safer than breeding. It would be some time before he tried that again! At least I had discovered one way of keeping numbers down.

Success was further confirmed one cold January afternoon while shooting on a nearby estate at the edge of a normally quiet byroad. A series of vermin drives by the keeper and his friends had been in progress during the morning in the adjoining woods, and eventually the team of guns reached the beat adjacent to where I lay concealed on a grassy bank, my 50-odd dead birds propped conspicuously not more than 40 yards from the road. The first of a long line of vehicles screeched to a halt upon spotting what appeared to be a large flock of semi-tame woodies gorging themselves on the tattered rape crop and totally ignoring the convoy of vehicles. In an instant the driver had jumped out, loaded a couple of cartridges and was preparing to conduct a great slaughter among the thickest patch of blue. As luck would have it the driver of the following vehicle knew better, and jumped from his car in equal haste to prevent what could have been a painful incident. A few seconds more and I, in the same position as the flock of hens I had blasted with both barrels, might have erupted from my camouflaged nets with a Homo sapiens equivalent of a great deal of flapping and squawking.

Although static dead bird decoys were really effective on most occasions, it was obvious at times that something was sadly lacking, and a few birds still had the annoying habit of giving them a wide berth without showing the slightest sign of having even noticed their stiff cousins on the ground below. The decoys differed from the real thing by their complete lack of movement. Watching pigeon in a flock, constant movement is very noticeable as birds continuously flutter about, leap-frogging over their fellow diners to reach a better spot. It is obviously a case of the other man's grass, or in this instance the other pigeon's clover or peas, being always greener: wood pigeon, like most of the human race, are seldom contented with what they already have and expend much unnecessary energy in the search for something better. But whatever the cause, even the slightest movement acts as a magnet on passing birds, and any that swoop to join a feeding flock trigger off an immediate chain reaction among those resting in nearby trees, digesting their ill-gotten gains before topping up once more. The flashing white wing bars of an alighting pigeon act as a powerful feeding stimulant, summoning all but the most replete of woodies to the dining table. I needed an effective means of simulating this action.

With this thought in mind I acquired a suitable length of sprung steel wire and began a series of test flights from my bedroom window which, to give the test area a touch of authenticity, overlooked the vegetable garden. The plan was to simulate a hungry bird swooping from a tree top (in this case the bedroom window) to the decoy pattern (a bed of lettuces), thus encouraging others in sight to follow suit, with obvious benefits to the day's bag.

One end of the steel wire was twisted firmly around the

window frame 20 feet above the vegetable patch. The wire was then stretched taut and fixed to a stake hammered into the lettuce bed. Having completed the initial setting up operation I noted with some amusement that my experiment was under careful scrutiny from a suspicious neighbour, an elderly lady who crouched in ill-concealed bewilderment behind a pair of net curtains in the house opposite. I could almost read her mind. What was the fool up to now? I had obviously taken leave of my senses again. She had always suspected it would happen, keeping a wary eye on me ever since I had practised the art of swinging a hawk lure for an imaginary bird of prey in the back garden. On that occasion she had watched spellbound as I twirled a pair of crow wings fixed to a leather bag around my head on a long cord, jerking, throwing and calling as my then illusory hawk dived in hot pursuit. From that moment on I was probably suspected of practising some sort of black magic ritual.

But I digress. Having prepared the flight path and landing area, I wired up a dead pigeon in a reasonably lifelike attitude, wings outstretched and tail fanned, fitting it by a wire loop to the tightened wire. In theory I would later tie a strong length of fishing line to the rear end of the suspended decoy, enabling it to be returned to the tree after each flight by means of a small pulley fixed on a convenient branch above. This would save having to climb the tree after each launching and allow the decoy to be controlled from the concealment of the hide beneath. The launching itself would be effected by simply releasing the line, allowing the force of gravity to complete the graceful gliding descent to the 'flock' below. All this no doubt sounds extremely complicated – probably because it was.

The maiden flight was not an unqualified success. Upon the decoy's release the first ten feet were covered with speed, but the slack in the wire guideline brought the descending bird to an abrupt and untimely halt six feet above a row of Webbs Wonderfuls. This looked most unnatural and its resemblance to a hungry pigeon intent on a free feast of juicy lettuces left much to the imagination. I tried again – and again. The nearest I could get to the desired effect was by further tightening the guideline and setting it at a considerably steeper angle. The results were startling: if anything, the bird appeared over keen to feed, burying itself beak first in a prime lettuce and remaining in a vertical posture like a crashed toy glider. Indeed, as the decoy sizzled into the depths of the lettuce bed there was a marked similarity to a kamikaze pilot diving to attack an enemy aircraft carrier. Crude indeed, but it was the best I could do.

The next outing to a pea field on the village outskirts provided an ideal opportunity to begin aerial field trials. The ten acres were bereft of cover except for a stand of tall oaks lining a dry ditch along one side, and the podding peas had taken a sound thrashing from swarms of hungry pigeon — after the latest attack the crop appeared to have just weathered a severe hailstorm. After scaling the oak nearest to the damaged area to erect the gliding apparatus, I set up the static decoys and hid myself among a bunch of bent-over elder saplings to await the raiders' return.

I was not waiting long. The first customer came beating low across the pea field, dead on course for the decoy area. Brimming with confidence I released the fishing line. The glider descended almost exactly six feet from its starting point, and remained apparently suspended in thin air despite repeated jerking on the line to dislodge it. Immediately behind was an absolute bird's nest of entangled fishing line, hopelessly and irretrievably entwined among a maze of twisted branches. Not surprisingly the incoming woodie sensed that something was amiss. Obeying the cardinal rule of wood pigeon preservation, it put at least two shotgun ranges between itself and its hovering relation before pulling out of an erratic aerial display, returning to where it had come from at a considerably greater speed to spread the word that all was not well.

The majority appeared, however, to take little heed, for a steady stream began arriving over the field, obviously on the lookout for a suitable spot to continue their pilfering. Any that came almost within range were turned away by the sight of a dead pigeon rocking to and fro in the breeze, so in desperation I wrenched it down, and used instead the far simpler method of throwing a dead bird from hide to decoys to simulate the alighting bird. To my surprise and delight the effect was much improved; the dead bird drew pigeon from all points of the compass with the flash of its wings as it fell. Shooting was fast and furious throughout the afternoon until the light began to fade, but by then I had accumulated a three-figure bag, a good number of which were directly due to the simple but effective launching method. Shouldering gun, empty cartridge bag, decoys and the enormous sack or pigeons, I slogged my way back to the van well pleased with the day's sport and my new discovery. The gliding apparatus? To the best of my knowledge its rusting remains are still suspended from a certain tall oak.

Other forms of decoy movement were possible. With a pair of metal fencing stakes shaped like large skewers with a ring at the top I devised a flapping decoy, which drew flighting pigeons like iron filings to a magnet. The stakes were placed on either side of a dead pigeon, three feet apart and in line with the leading edge of the outspread wings. A length of fishing line salvaged from the last experiment was attached to each wing tip, joined in front of the bird and controlled from inside the hide. A few sharp tugs on the line at the appropriate moment caused the wings to flap in a most alluring manner, enticing even the most stubborn of woodies to its doom.

Next in importance to the decoy in any ardent decoyer's equipment is a good portable hide. As pigeon are far from being short-sighted some form of concealment is an obvious necessity. An effective screen can often be erected in a favourable position within range of the decoy pattern from local materials found on site, particularly during the summer months when vegetation is lush and abundant, but in winter, when the trees and bushes have shed their foliage, cover is a scarce commodity. Straw bales are an ideal solution in some positions, being warm, windproof and extremely comfortable, though the pigeon needs time to get accustomed to them when sited in exposed areas. Another failing with this type of hide is its lack of portability. As an absolute minimum of a dozen is required to erect a good working model, the hide must be accurately sited, since there is nothing more frustrating than to see pigeon streaming into another part of the field while you sit watching the action from inside a comfortable and carefully built construction overlooking a flock of redundant decoys. You are then faced with the difficult decision of either wasting an hour humping a dozen rain-soaked sponges across half a mile of often muddy countryside – probably upsetting the pigeon in the process – or simply giving up and returning home empty-handed. Either way, I found it far easier to study the pigeons' movements and erect the hide correctly in the first place.

I spent quite a few of my early pigeon shooting days with a couple of friends in a very palatial bale hide that would almost have passed as a decent-sized strawstack. It was complete with all mod cons including seats, lookout holes and a parrafin stove on which we warmed our hands and cooked our Sunday lunches of tinned beans and apple dumplings. Sadly, oil stoves and straw bales just did not mix. On frequent occasions we inadvertently set fire to the hide and it became necessary to get out with all speed. This also defeated our objective. Wet straw smokes something akin to wet rags: it was often difficult even to see an approaching pigeon through the dense, eye-stinging smoke screen, let alone shoot it. Even if our bags were small, though, we at least caused enough confusion to scare the pigeon and keep the crops free from their attentions for a short while.

The most portable – and possibly the coldest – winter hide can be erected in a matter of minutes from a couple of ex-army camouflage nets draped over a set of vertical poles, the nets being interwoven with armfuls of dead grass and other local materials found on site to blend them into the immediate surroundings. Equally if not more important is the actual siting of the hide in relation to the decoy pattern, preferably in easy range but well downwind of the decoys. Pigeon paying a visit invariably turn into the wind prior to alighting, therefore passing in range of the downwind hide en route and providing the concealed shooter with more opportunities to fill the bag.

The importance of choosing a favourable spot, though for a quite different reason, was once demonstrated to me in no uncertain terms. Having spent the best part of 20 minutes constructing a roomy and, as I thought, comfortable affair in the dividing hedge of two pea fields, sited directly beneath a strong flightline, I was somewhat surprised to discover that my hide housed a wasp's nest, which had an equally strong if not even stronger flightline. To keep the wasps busy until I was safely out of their way I trod in the entrance hole to prevent those inside from emerging. Eager to begin shooting I completely forgot about those already outside the nest, going about their everyday business of spoiling fruit crops, collecting food and stinging people. They returned with monotonous regularity to jog my memory!

I discovered another effective form of hide in the machan, or tree hide. A stout platform can be constructed in any suitable tree on the pigeon's flightline or overlooking the decoy pattern, and the machan can often prove extremely productive in terms of sport in all seasons of the year. Its main advantage over the ground-level hide lies in the fact that many birds, wood pigeon included, are often put on the alert by any unusual new feature in an exposed position at ground level, where obvious signs of an ambush will send them wheeling away to safer regions. I found the majority of wildlife completely oblivious of a hide in a tree, and birds often alighted a few feet from where I perched or clung concealed, never expecting to discover a human being waiting in ambush among the ivy-covered branches of an oak or the dense swaying boughs of a tall Scots pine. Indeed, one of the most interesting aspects of the machan is the pleasure of being able to observe a variety of wild creatures at very close range, literally a bird's eye view of wildlife in its own element. A cock blackbird may come to pour out its liquid and melodious song six feet above your head, a bewildered little owl attempt to perch on your gun barrel or a tiny treecreeper search a craggy tree trunk – or your cord trousers – for a beakful of insects.

By no means all my observations from a tree hide, however, have been concerned with wildlife in the usual meaning of the word. At a farmer's request I had arrived at noon one day ready to set up shop, hoping to make an inroad into a vast concentration of woodies intent on feeding in a large pea field. From the safety angle the spot chosen by the pigeon for their feast was a good one, with not so much as a small bush or tangle of undergrowth anywhere near to conceal a gun, except a lone oak tree supporting a generous growth of thick ivy. Watching the wood pigeons' move through binoculars, I noticed that the tree was continually used as a perching place by new arrivals, which pitched into the top branches before gliding down to feed with their companions on the ground. Thus encouraged, I put the flock to flight and quickly set up shop on the worst attacked area, climbing the tree to overlook the decoys from an ideal and sturdy platform of interwoven ivy boughs. Two hours and several cartridges later the pigeon were arriving in a steady stream and I began nurturing hopes of a three-figure bag. They were not to be fulfilled.

Presently a battered Morris Minor drew to a halt in the field gateway and from it stepped, of all things, a courting couple who, amid much lively banter, headed immediately in my direction for the shade of the old oak tree. Feeling rather silly perched in the oak like an overweight pigeon, I remained silent and still in the hope that they would pass by and leave me in peace. In pigeon terms they billed and cooed directly beneath my lofty perch for the best part of half an hour. Luckily that was all, for he was substantially larger than I and there were quite enough laid peas in the area already without a further rolled area to add to the farmer's loss. To add to my frustration the pigeon now really went to town, pouring over the distant hedge in a continual stream towards me, but veering sharply away as they spotted the pair below the tree. It was apparently an equally frustrating venture for the male half of the courting couple. Suffice it to say that when they eventually retired I fired at the next three pigeon without touching a feather.

During winter afternoons the machan can be successfully employed to intercept the main flightlines of a favourite roosting

wood, providing much excitement as the pigeon arrive to seek warmth and shelter for the night. Part of the excitement, though, comes from the thrill of discovering just how long one can defy the laws of gravity as one clings tenaciously to a 40-foot pine during a winter gale. Always providing that one remains aloft, the main advantage one has as a tree-top shooter over one's earth-bound counterpart is a view unrestricted by a maze of branches when roost-shooting in a wood, thus enabling clear shots to be taken instead of attempting to blast one's way through a canopy of interwoven twigs. The highest flighting pigeon are also a good deal closer, allowing one to bag birds well out of range from ground level. But from my own limited experience I can verify that the machan is not for the weak-willed or faint-hearted – nor, it would seem, for the easily embarrassed!

It was sometimes necessary to resort to the complete opposite of the machan, namely a dugout hide which came into its own on large fields completely devoid of cover. Excavating what looked like a grave in the eerie half-light of dawn often aroused a certain amount of suspicion from casual passers by and farm labourers off to work, but the dugout more than proved its worth in wide-open areas where other more conventional forms of con-cealment were nonexistent. On my best day from a dugout I amassed well over 200 pigeon from a vast field of frozen pota-toes, having dug a three-foot square hole and covered it with camouflage nets and potato haulms, squatting within to shoot through a small hole left overlooking the decoys. A tractor driver provided me with much amusement, cultivating at the far end of the field and gaping open-mouthed as pigeon after pigeon bit the dust apparently several hundred yards from the nearest cover sufficient to conceal a human. I heightened his astonishment by continually appearing and disappearing to and from the very bowels of the earth, as frequent picking up was necessary to avoid the decoy area looking like the inside of a game dealer's plucking shed.

My crop protection duties steadily expanded to such an extent and area of ground that I was shooting almost every day and detonating an incredibly high number of cartridges during the peak periods of crop damage. In one particular week alone my stock was depleted by over 1,400 shells, the bag amounting to well in excess of 1,000 pigeon. The outlay required to maintain a regular supply of such proportions was having a really crippling effect on my weekly wage, despite the sale of pigeon, so much so in fact that I began to consider the possibility of loading my own cartridges, a process reputed almost to halve the cost of ammunition.

I eventually invested in a machine of American manufacture, prompted by such descriptions as 'faultless', 'foolproof' and 'easy to understand', which the advertisement in a shooting magazine frequently used when referring to its evidently simple and straightforward operating instructions. Having always been a victim of Murphy's Law I was quite aware of the fact that if there was a wrong way of doing the job I would doubtless discover it. Gunpowder, which came complete with the obvious dangers of high explosive, would not allow for too many mistakes, and it had to be treated with due respect for its lively qualities. Bearing this in mind I bought the machine and set up a small-scale ammunition factory in the garden shed, preparing the various components in a neat and orderly manner and following the loading instructions with meticulous care to the very last grain of powder and pellet of shot. It was all quite simple really. I could not think why I had not thought of it before. Soon I had 50 primed charges finished, but before producing more I decided to conduct a few field tests to ensure the effectiveness of my prototype home-loads.

To say they were of mixed ballistic qualities would have been a considerable understatement. Although a few reduced their victims to nothing more than a mass of tattered skin and bone, others, even at almost point-blank range, appeared to have no effect, hardly possessing the velocity of a damp squib. A shooting acquaintance tested a few sample rounds, despite my warning that I could accept none of the responsibility if he should inadvertently blow himself up. Much to my relief he later returned in one piece but remarked that my prototypes were well below par, coupling this with the unlikely boast that he could spit further than the average range of my shot charge.

Taking his advice I applied more pressure when inserting the wax column and recrimping the end, thus attempting to ensure a more potent loading. The results were much better although I occasionally disproved the claim for the machine's foolproof qualities despite having the loading schedule firmly in my mind. Decap, recap, load powder, seat wads, load shot and crimp the end, that was all there was to it. Quite a simple procedure to remember. Somewhere along the line I once omitted to add the powder charge, the effects of which were rather tiresome. The cartridge went off with a restricted 'phutt', after which the shot charge trickled ominously from the muzzle end and a pigeon with a very charmed life jinked away, rocking from side to side in apparent hysterics. I was left with the frustrating task of removing a stubborn wad column from the blocked barrel, a process carried out with a slender hazel bough and a great deal of patience, both scarce commodities in a remote straw bale hide; and my exasperation was heightened by an almost endless stream of pigeon that had been awaiting this very moment to drop in for a snack. In place of the usual barrage of lead, incoming birds were greeted with nothing worse than a descriptive vocal onslaught which they proceeded to ignore, hovering temptingly around the decoy area like a swarm of Large White butterflies over a cabbage patch. It was some time before I made that mistake again.

5

Ospreys to Alligators

I have always been something of a collector. The urge to hoard was strong within me from the first and it had not been long before the first of a succession of passions had begun with that coveted possession of many a small country boy; a collection of wild birds' eggs all neatly cleaned, blown and presented in a box lined with fine sawdust. The practice of oology is now quite rightly frowned upon by naturalists, myself included, besides being highly illegal, but in those far-off days I knew no better and spent a great deal of my spare time searching the hedgerows, woods and marshy places where a wide variety of nests could be expected.

Besides being educational and pleasing to the eye, eggs of all descriptions were always much sought after as a primitive form of currency between schoolmates. Thus a magpie's egg could often be swapped for half a dozen marbles, a crow's egg was worth at least a sherbet dip, and the greeny-brown eggs of the jay, by virtue of the difficulties involved in finding their well-hidden nests, became almost priceless. Harmful though it undoubtedly was, at least I always restricted myself to taking only one specimen to further my collection from any clutch of eggs, except in the case of magpies, jays, crows and other pests, which themselves caused far more harm than I, indiscriminately plundering any nest of eggs or nestlings as a tasty addition to their diet.

Of the three pests the magpie was by far the most common, seen regularly along the hedgerows and skipping from tree to tree, its pied plumage flashing black and white as it chattered and swore nineteen to the dozen. Its huge nest was unmistakable, built amongst the top branches of the very thickest bushes, usually blackthorn, and constructed of a mass of interwoven sticks cemented firmly in place with beakfuls of thick mud which dried to a concrete-like consistency. This veritable fortress was topped with a heavy thatching of twigs, leaving a small magpie-sized entrance hole on one side. From this it could defend its nest from virtually anything with its stabbing beak – anything, that was, except a small horror intent on separating it from a clutch of blotched eggs with which to purchase catapult ammunition.

Having removed the sitting tenant with a few well-placed missiles, often the only way of transporting the eggs from the nest without fear of breakage was to carry them in my mouth, two at a time, which left both hands free to aid the difficult and often painful descent from the thorn bush. As the magpie usually lays five or six eggs, three journeys to and from the nest were normally necessary to collect the entire clutch and by the time the job was accomplished I began to feel like an inflamed pin-cushion. Only once did I make the mistake of trying to save time by carrying three eggs in my mouth at the same time, an experiment never repeated. Shinning down the twisted tree trunk my chin connected with a jutting horizontal bough, snapping my jaws together with distasteful results. Magpie omelette, especially in an advanced state of incubation and containing the brittle shells, is not a delicacy to be highly regarded. It joined the greater part of my breakfast at the bottom of the tree.

In one magpie's nest I discovered something quite different from the expected clutch of eggs. Forcing my arm through the small entrance hole my hand came briefly into contact with something warm and furry. Besides being furry it was also furious, for out popped the largest stoat I had ever set eyes on, giving me the fright of my life and making a hurried beeline for the earth below, displaying a climbing ability usually reserved for members of the squirrel family. I never discovered just what the stoat was doing several feet above its normal terrestrial element. It had probably raided the nest for a tasty meal of eggs or chicks, or perhaps had retired to the lofty retreat for a quiet snooze. Nothing would have induced me to put my hands inside that particular nest again, and anyway being unable to defy the laws of gravity, I failed to remain in the tree long enough to have tried if I had wanted to. One thing I did discover – a much faster but more painful way of descending from a thorn bush.

Falling down trees was not the only drawback of my hobby by a long chalk. I was frequently 'bombed' from the air while visiting nesting sites, as the state of my school cap would testify. In many creatures it is a natural reaction to disgorge food or evacuate the bowels when deeply disturbed, thus effectively lightening the payload when a fast escape is the order of the day. This practice was invariably carried out by brooding birds immediately upon leaving the nest site, with the inevitable result that anything below was usually a sitting target for waste matter. Owls were among the worst offenders, usually remaining in their nesting holes until I arrived directly below and then bursting out suddenly with bomb doors well and truly open.

An old hollow tree near our house was the regular nesting site for a beautiful pair of barn owls. Each year the birds returned to set up home at the base of a deep twisting tunnel that dropped several feet to a cushion of rotting wood pulp and a few dead leaves inside the oak, there to raise their family of comical black-eyed owlets of varying sizes, which were a constant source of interest to me. This owl, besides being wise, was also renowned for its aiming abilities. With the accuracy of a Trafalgar Square pigeon, nine times out of ten it caught me squarely across the face when flitting from the exit hole like a huge white moth, its mutes streaming hot and smelly as if from a running tap. The occupants of a nearby heronry were almost as accurate, but if the barn owl's faeces resembled a running tap, the herons' were equivalent to a burst water main. Still, it was supposed to be lucky.

It was while visiting the heronry that I discovered another of the heron's rather disgusting habits. One easily accessible nest in a tall fir contained four well-grown youngsters, which I used to visit regularly to observe their growth rate and watch them turn from rather grotesque bundles of legs, beak and skin into elegant and very graceful creatures, which stood immobile on the edge of the huge nesting platform until closely approached. When in range of their long necks great care was necessary to avoid a stabbing dagger-like bill connecting with my face with the speed of a striking cobra. As the birds reached maturity they assumed the habits of their parents, evacuating any excess weight in readiness for flight. On one occasion I clambered to the nesting platform soon after the youngsters had been fed, and peering over the edge of the bowl was ceremoniously presented with the contents of the larger bird's crop; a partially digested frog. This was regurgitated and deposited in a steaming and evil-smelling mess down the front of my shirt, almost causing me to follow suit with the remains of my breakfast.

The eggs of moorhen were collected for another purpose. They were delicious. In the springtime father and I would search the river-bank vegetation and overgrown drainage channels to find the nesting platforms, often cunningly sited over the water or on patches of deep and dangerous marsh mud well out of reach from the bank. To overcome this we tied a large dessert spoon to the end of a long stick, which enabled us to lift the eggs safely. Before picking up a full clutch, the first had to be tested in water to see whether it was fresh laid or partly incubated. Those that sank in water were deemed satisfactory for collection, but 'floaters' were returned to the nest; they floated because the airspace inside the egg had enlarged with incubation. I have never seen or tasted another egg with such a rich yolk of a brilliant orange colour. The sight of a clutch of moorhens eggs in the frying pan would cause many a battery hen to hang her head in shame.

Egg collecting, for obvious reasons, could only be carried out during the relatively short season of late spring and early summer, and it was not long before I sought to discover a project that would occupy the endless long hot summer days of the school holidays. The answer came one bright morning as I was crossing a small meadow on my way to commence battle with a large shoal of perch recently discovered in a deep region on a bend in the river. As I walked, a constant cloud of brilliant and beautiful butterflies danced dizzily around me in the warm July sun, alighting delicately behind me on the rich carpet of marsh plants and flowers. The Small Copper, gaudily clad in the glittering hue from which its name was derived, paused briefly to sample the star-like flowers of the daisy patch, and the Meadow Brown, much commoner but less likely to attract attention in her sober garb, deposited a cargo of light-green eggs on the stems of the taller grasses. Peacocks, Red Admirals, Blues and Brimstones, all were found and recognised, each adding fuel to the fire that was beginning to smoulder within me – for a collection of butterflies and moths.

But first things first. I needed equipment. According to the book the basic requirements were cheap and readily obtainable, and many could be home-made or improvised. In a few days I was almost ready. A tiddler net which had long been obsolete was brought out of retirement and I made a rather crude pegging board from a thin plank, on which to mount any victims to complete the drying process necessary for preservation. Mother

supplied a selection of pins, together with an empty cutlery canteen lined with green baize in which to house my collection. All I needed was a killing bottle. The book recommended the use of cyanide or ammonia as the most effective killing agent, but as the lady assistant in the chemist's shop would not entrust a nasty little boy with a bottle of ammonia for killing butterflies, and cyanide gas was obviously out of the question, I was forced to resort to a cruder method; crushed laurel leaves sealed in an airtight jar. Although somewhat slower in taking effect, the book recommended this for the 'painless and happy dispatch' of all winged insects from a Limespeck Pug to an Elephant Hawkmoth.

Thereafter I was always to be found wielding my net in any likely looking butterfly habitat, though I soon discovered that there was a definite art in bringing the elusive and beautiful creatures to hand. Haphazard sweeping of the net at selected specimens in flight rarely proved effective and my first assault of vicious swipes only served to chop down a formerly immaculate Peacock, neatly halved by the rim of the net and collapsing to earth. To make things easier, and realising that the finished article would look far more presentable if mounted whole rather than in a collection of pieces, I evolved a less strenuous approach; dropping the net carefully over them as they paused to rest or sample nectar from a flower. This proved to be a more rewarding system of capture and by the end of the summer holidays I had caught, dispatched, preserved and mounted a colourful and comprehensive display to grace the inside of the cutlery box, all neatly named and labelled in my best handwriting.

When the butterflies ceased their activities for the day, moth hunting came into its own, and there were even more species of these to acquire – something approaching 2,500 in the British Isles, if the tiny micro-moths are taken into consideration. Most dark nights would find me cavorting around outside with torch and net, searching the outsides of illuminated windows for any new specimens drawn to the light. I also worked a trap made from a torch in a box, where moths attracted to the beam made a one-way journey along a short length of drainpipe used to funnel them into a box. There, next morning, amongst what seemed like thousands of droning mosquitoes and a seething mass of night-flying beetles, I occasionally secured an odd specimen or two for the collection, though the cost of torch batteries was prohibitive in relation to what I caught.

A more interesting way of obtaining moths was to collect their larvae and pupae, the former being kept in large jam-jars topped up with regular supplies of their favourite food plants until, gorged to repletion, they would transform into pupae in readiness for the magical metamorphosis to the adult moth to take place. It caused me great excitement to see them eventually hatching out, as the greater number were unknown to me in the larval stage and it was always a thrill to discover just what new species I had managed to acquire. It also never ceased to amaze me that such perfect and beautiful creatures could emerge from the maggot-like pupal case, and it often seemed a great pity they were destined for the killing bottle prior to mounting on pins and final installation in the cutlery box.

At the end of each season of butterfly and moth collecting my case of trophies was stored in a dark cupboard for the duration of the winter. It was often some time before I again opened the lid. One spring I was hardly able to believe my eyes. The butterflies were no longer things of great beauty and my moths were distinctly moth-eaten! Returning to the book I read a small chapter on the necessary steps needed to guard against the attacks of mite and other undesirable aliens, and this made the explanation all too plain. My collection had suffered the depredations of microscopic beetle larvae, *Anthrenus scrophulariae* and *Demestes lardarius*, to be more accurate. The Latin terminology, however, was not a patch on the names I called the infernal little creatures. The fruits of many summer projects had been completely destroyed.

From the trials and tribulations of entomology I advanced to something more solid and permanent, namely a collection of bones. I often came across the skeletal remains of bird and beast about the fields, bones bleached white by the action of sun and rain, which in time destroyed all but the skeleton, leaving the remains completely clean to form the basis of my new craze. The skull was obviously the most desirable part of any skeleton found, displaying much of the character of the living creature and giving a good indication of its main diet and the methods evolved for securing or disposing of its food. The skulls of fox or stoat, for instance, display a pair of well-developed canine teeth for catching and killing prey as food, while that of a coypu, a fairly strict vegetarian, holds an impressive set of huge orange incisors with which it gnaws a living among the succulent plants of river-side and marsh. Browsing and grazing animals, such as deer, cattle, goats and the like, are another example; they have well-developed rows of back teeth or molars, which are extremely efficient tools for grinding grass and other tough vegetation when the animal retreats to a secluded spot to chew the cud, after quickly taking its fill from an exposed, and therefore dangerous, position. Birds can also be classified by the same system. The thin bill of the insectivorous feeder enables it to prise out insects and larvae from the craggiest of tree trunks; the wide, often serrated spatula of a duck is cleverly fashioned to filter food from water and the long bills of wading birds are equipment to probe the muddy regions of marsh and estuary for their daily rations.

There was much to be studied and learned from my latest hobby and it was all very interesting – for me at least. At school the science mistress encouraged my activities, but a weakness for skeletons did little to promote my relationships with the more squeamish of my classmates. During the science period I was often involved in the process of cleaning, sorting out and setting up of various bodies. One never-to-be-forgotten morning I took a dead cat to school, found mangled in a road-side ditch and obviously the victim of a passing car. I had kept a covetous eye on the cat for several days, allowing the maggots to hasten the cleaning process but hoping nobody would pick it up before me (though it was difficult to imagine what anyone else would want with a dead cat). By the time the body was collected in a carrier bag it was in what might be described as a fairly advanced state of decomposition. Needless to say I was not the most popular passenger on the school bus that morning. Two hours of central heating did nothing to alleviate the deceased's aroma before the science lesson, and by the time I literally let the cat out of the bag a definite pong wafted thickly around the science laboratory.

My studies progressed quite well for some time and on odd occasions I was even beginning to enjoy my lessons at school,

until one morning I went a shade too far in my attempts to terrorise one of the girls in my class. With hopes of missing yet another period of boring book-work, I had trapped a house mouse for dissecting which, with any luck, would occupy at least the bulk of the science lesson. At that time I was rather fond of one particular girl. During the midmorning break we stood chatting and flirting in the laboratory waiting for the lesson to begin. As she turned away from me my glance fell – quite easily, I must admit – to the open neck of her shirt. Aha, something said to me, just the place for a mouse! Almost without thinking and possibly prompted beyond all reason by the prospect of being asked to retrieve it, I took the mouse from my pocket and popped it down the neck of her shirt. Poor girl: it must have been a horrifying experience, at least if her hysterics were anything to go by. It was a new experience for me also, since I had never before seen or heard a member of the opposite sex scream at the top of her voice for five solid minutes, as I frantically attempted to recover what was left of my mouse, furthering my education on the subject of anatomy into the bargain. As might be expected, it was not long before a teacher came to investigate the sudden and alarming outburst. To cut a long and painful story short, my research during school hours was instantly and indefinitely curtailed. I spent the next few minutes studying the interior of the headmaster's office and wondering whether to take up stamp-collecting.

It is very strange indeed how some chance incident in the course of our lives often eventually leads to something much bigger, perhaps opening a new door on an interest that is to play a large part in our whole way of life in future years. One particular incident that occurred when I was fifteen years old sticks vividly in my mind, and I often reflect upon the interests and opportunities that I would probably never have enjoyed had it not happened, and of a splendid old Norfolk character I would never have had the pleasure of meeting.

On this particular occasion I was, accompanied by two close friends, enjoying a few hours' pigeon shooting on a cold and windy January morning. We had been guarding a field of kale since the sun had risen like a huge fried egg over the distant woods, and were concealed in a warm bale hide at the edge of the tattered crop, which had been shredded unmercifully by a swarm of pigeon over the preceding few days. By midmorning we had accounted for quite a number of birds as they arrived to gorge on the sweet tops of the kale, when Ken, my companion in magpie shooting, spotted a rabbit bolting from the nearby hedge, ears laid flat across its back and racing in obvious terror across a strip of barley stubble, where it squatted beside a tussock of grass on the open ground. With thoughts of adding a bonus to the bag we crept silently from the comforts of the hide and made our way along the bare hedgerow to where the rabbit lay concealed. Before we reached it a stoat burst from the hedge, nose to the ground and obviously hot on the scent of its hidden quarry. Seeing us it immediately dashed back to the safety of the hedge, robbed of the chance of an easy breakfast. The rabbit remained hidden until we were within easy range and was rolled over as it bolted full pelt the way it had come.

After picking it up we returned to the hide to continue our sport with the pigeons, but a few minutes later the very same thing happened again. Another full-grown rabbit popped out of the hedge close by the hide, just in range of my other friend, Ron, who rolled it over with his second barrel. Almost immediately a streak of brown fury charged from the hedge, jumped onto the rabbit's back and bit it behind the ears. It was not going to be deprived of its breakfast again. The stoat had completely ignored the two shots fired at the rabbit, so intent was it on securing a meal at last. My hurried shot found its mark and the stoat lay beside the dead rabbit, its mask even in death set in a wicked snarl.

On closer examination it was found to be in exceptionally good order, a perfect specimen with not so much as a bullet-hole showing to spoil its appearance. I decided there and then to get it preserved as a reminder of its suicidal behaviour. But where did one find a taxidermist? The local museum, where a magnificent display of wildlife adorns several huge rooms in Norwich Castle, seemed the likely place to begin enquiries. In answer to a phone call I was at once recommended to seek out a gentleman by the name of Fred Ashton, who lived and worked at his home in Larkman Lane on the outskirts of Norwich. I put the stoat in a cool place and a letter of enquiry brought a reply several days later (by which time the stoat was beginning to get a trifle high), requesting me to forward the body with all haste before decomposition worsened.

I packaged the stoat as instructed, plugging the mouth with a large wad of cotton wool to absorb any blood or moisture and prevent it from seeping out to contaminate the skin. The rear orifice was treated in much the same manner, though with considerably greater dexterity and respect. Thus suitably topped and tailed it was popped into a cardboard box and I set off to the post office to catch the last collection. I was not to be rid of it easily. As usual just before closing time a large queue had formed near the postal counter and I resigned myself to having to wait for some considerable time, while each customer poured out the events of the last few days to the busy postmistress. After absorbing a few minutes of local gossip I began to notice a faint but familiar odour hanging on the air around me. At once I recognised the smell — it was my stoat!

During the rather rough handling it had received in packaging I must have unwittingly disturbed the extremely volatile scent glands of the animal. A sideways glance at the other customers in the queue made it abundantly clear that I was not the only one possessed of a sharp nose. The lady directly behind me cautiously inspected her shoes, probably fearing that she had literally fallen foul of one of the local dogs as she crossed the village green, and one or two of the others glanced in silent suspicion at their companions in the queue. The smell of a dead stoat in the very restricted area of a small country post office has to be experienced to be believed, and I breathed (although cautiously) a sigh of relief as my turn at the counter came. The post mistress received my parcel without question, transferring it to the scales to check the postage.

'That's rather heavy for such a small parcel', she commented with a wrinkle of her nose and in a manner that invited me to reveal the contents. She failed to mention that the air immediately surrounding the package was a good deal heavier, and my noncommital nod did nothing to relieve her curiosity. I paid the stamp fee in haste and gratefully excused myself.

A month later a letter arrived to say the stoat was finished and ready for collection and I set out, guided by rather vague directions, to call on Mr Ashton. It was late in the evening and already becoming dark as I finally arrived outside number 39, Larkman Lane; a small detached bungalow set in a miniature forest of over-grown garden. There was no sign of life as I banged loudly on the peeling front door, and no welcome chink of light shone through the roughly boarded-up windows. The place looked absolutely deserted. I decided to try the back door. After negotiating something of an obstacle course of old bikes, wooden frames and bits and pieces of discarded furniture, I eventually noticed a faint glimmer of light exuding from the glass-panelled back door. A shadow materialised in the glass frame as I knocked, lit by a dim light from behind. It appeared to be slightly stooped and shuffling with some difficulty to reach the back door. The battered door creaked open on its rusty hinges and a face, almost as weatherbeaten, furrowed and peeling as the door itself, peered out into the darkness of the night.

'Mr Ashton?' I enquired politely. 'I've come to collect my stoat.'

'Come in, come in', answered the face, quickly sizing up the situation. 'That is,' he added as an afterthought, 'if you can get in.'

He was not joking, for as I squeezed through the half-open door I saw the reason for his earlier difficulties in reaching the door. The room was absolutely crammed full of preserved specimens. I gazed in awe at the spectacle before me. Every part of the room was filled to saturation point with a veritable kaleidoscope of natural colour, row upon row of magnificently preserved birds, animals and fish of every conceivable size, shape and colour. Each piece of sagging furniture held its quota. The large table which doubled as a workbench was filled to overflowing and a sideboard stood almost unrecognisable beneath a radiance of flowing plumes. To me it was paradise.

'Watch he doesn't pick you', warned Fred as I squeezed past a two-foot square wire cage, taking great care not to tread on a dozing cat that lay among the crumpled folds of a hessian sack. The cage at my elbow contained a mischievous looking carrion crow, his head cocked on one side, wicked black eyes glinting in the light, eagerly awaiting his chance for a thrust at any part of my anatomy if and when I was foolish enough to provide him with the opportunity. Crow obviously enjoyed residing near the back door, where the chances of finding an unsuspecting victim were much greater. Eventually, knowing that Fred's warning had robbed him of an easy victim, he settled down to preen in the far corner of his cage.

Fred somewhat remarkably managed to produce a chair from the mass of accumulated work and, after I had settled up with him for the stoat, he resumed work on a skin he had been in the process of cleaning when I arrived. The skin, I was informed, belonged to a female sparrowhawk, but at that particular moment its resemblance to the living bird left much to the imagination. I had never seen one inside out before. It looked nothing so much as a mass of twisted skin, a few dangling bones and odd patches of barred feathers. Fred was in the process of cleaning all traces of flesh from its skull, and in due course he opened up a small hole in the back of the skull.

'I often pick m' brains', he beamed, removing a large blob of grey matter with the tip of a knife, leaving a clean, round cavity that had served as a brainbox. As we talked, he worked almost automatically with practised and nimble fingers, glancing at his work now and again to make sure all was going according to plan. He had, it transpired, started his long career with the old-time firm of Norwich taxidermists founded by Thomas Gunn, who, when the trade was in its heyday and in great demand by collectors, was the proprietor of a shop devoted solely to the ancient art. Working from St Giles, Gunn's had achieved country-wide fame – a reputation well deserved if the specimens I later saw were of the normal standard. Alas, as with so many of the old-time crafts, taxidermy became unfashionable and the shop had finally to be closed down, leaving Fred without a job. But he retained and increased his skills and it was not long before he decided to go into business on his own, thus keeping alive a trade and an all-absorbing interest which he was never to regret.

While Fred related some of his past history I studied part of the varied contents of the room. Peacocks, pheasants, woodpeckers, kingfishers, waterfowl and waders and countless others all seemed to be represented in some form or another, each tastefully mounted in a natural pose and possessing a life and beauty that would remain for years to come.

My glance fell on the cat I had almost succeeded in standing on just after my arrival. It had not moved. It was apparently asleep, and I was half expecting to hear it purr. It was impossible for my unpractised eye to tell whether it was stuffed or alive, but eventually my curiosity got the better of me.

'Is it stuffed?'

Fred grinned back. I was obviously not the first to enquire. With a twinkle in his eye he invited me to pick it up and stroke it. I did. It was as stiff as a board!

Fred then produced another cat, this time a huge ginger tom. Unlike its dozing relation it had been mounted in a particularly ferocious attitude, crouching low to the ground like a stalking tiger, mouth open in a silent snarl and legs tucked back as if preparing to spring at an imaginary prey. The bushy tail was curled snake-like, adding greatly to an overall display of aggression. One thing troubled me. The open-fronted case in which it crouched did it little justice, looking in a sadly dilapidated and weatherbeaten state of repair. The cat was not for sale, explained Fred, as he had mounted it for a special purpose. Although in a temporary state of redundancy during the winter months, it would resume its job in the spring, silently but effectively guarding Fred's rows of prize peas and other vegetables and keeping them free from the attentions of raiding sparrows.

All too soon it was time for me to leave. Collecting my stoat, I bade Fred goodnight, after promising him (and myself) that I would return. In fact I returned time and time again to spend many an interesting evening with the old character, and each time Fred managed to conjure up some new specimen to show me or some tale to relate of years gone by. I asked him how many creatures resided with him in the tiny bungalow, but Fred admitted that he had no idea, as he could never find the time or the patience to carry out the mammoth task of counting them. The rest of the bungalow, he informed me, housed a similar quantity of creatures to his workroom, and to prove the point I was taken on a conducted tour of what must have surely qualified as being one of the smallest wildlife museums in the country.

Fred had not exaggerated; in fact, quite the reverse. The rest of the dwelling appeared to hold an even greater density of work than the workshop itself. Along the dim and narrow hallway, suitably garnished with a number of stuffed bats, a magnificent osprey in full flight clasped a freshly killed roach in its powerful talons, overshadowing a collection of gulls, waders and pheasants. There was barely space to pass through the 'sitting room', but the effort was well rewarded. Here it was all too plain to see why Fred had never managed to assess the extent of his sitting tenants. The large room was full to overflowing with his work, much of it sadly gathering dust as it waited for an owner that never returned to collect it. An evil-looking alligator, all of six feet long, took up a considerable amount of floor area, regarding us with a spine-chilling glare as we surveyed the room. Otters, fox cubs, reed- and vegetation-filled cases of fish, fowl and mammals watched us with glassy and unblinking stare, some appearing aggressive and threatening, others docile and playful, each displaying the mood and expression relevant to the attitude in which the skin had been mounted. The doleful and begging eyes of a seal pup, the crafty deliberation of a hunting fox or the proud aloofness of a bird of prey – each seemed to portray an expression befitting its character and lifestyle to perfection.

But more was to come. If the largest room in the house was overcrowded, the smallest room was the *pièce de résistance*. On the edge of what appeared to be Fred's bath, a heron poised delicately on the wide rim behind the taps, to all intents keeping a silent vigil for any signs of a fish to appear in the region of the plughole. The chances of this happening were not as remote as one might expect, for the bath already contained two huge pike from the Norfolk Broads, both weighing on the heavy side of 30 pounds and awaiting transfer to a glass case. Although much tempted I refrained from asking Fred how and where he carried out his own ablutions. I myself have never been a great lover of bath water, and even without that fact I am sure nothing would have induced me to share the bathtub with its two piscatorial inhabitants – each, I might add, armed with several rows of razor-sharp teeth.

6

Moorhen to Mayhem

As my visits to see Fred became more frequent, very soon I began to amass quite a collection of preserved wildlife. My bedroom was in danger of resembling his overcrowded bungalow, as I often picked up dead bodies along the roads or shot something that looked far too good to eat.

For some time it puzzled me why Fred was always keen to find out exactly how a specimen had died, and I presently learned that he had another minor interest centred on his work. As the majority of bodies brought to him were of necessity in a fresh and clean condition, he often supplemented his daily bread with anything that looked even remotely edible. To Fred meat was meat, whether it was deer or dormouse, wild duck or woodpecker. He took great delight in sampling any new species, adding its delicate flavour to his already comprehensive range of culinary experiences. My visits all too often coincided with his food-sampling trials. Thus I was somewhat reluctantly introduced to the delights of, among other dishes, mute swan, pike, fallow deer and some other tough odd-tasting flesh of which Fred would not reveal the true identity – in case, he explained, I should turn green at the very thought of having consumed it with such relish. I suspect it was badger, as there was a freshly mounted specimen standing on his workbench at the time. Fred was like that.

Actually, the mute swan was not too bad, having some of the flavour and much of the toughness of an under-hung goose, but the pike was anything but a delicacy.

'Quite good, isn't it?' ventured Fred, watching my expression closely as I chewed . . . and chewed . . . and chewed.

'Well, at least it's different', I replied.

Different was indeed the word for it. I had never before attempted to consume what seemed like a wad of cotton wool stuffed with pins. However, I drew the line at otter stew, a self-explanatory dish which Fred informed me was quite delicious. I excused myself from that rather dubious pleasure by assuring Fred that I had just finished my evening meal.

Much of Fred's boundless enthusiasm inevitably rubbed off on many of those that had the pleasure of meeting him. The thing that most impressed me was his untiring interest in the display of natural beauty that is to be found in all the wild places. Despite his 60-odd years he was every bit as keen to learn something new as a young schoolboy on his first nature ramble, travelling the entire county on an ancient bicycle searching the roadsides for casualties of passing cars, and collecting anything of interest in a large handle-bar basket. Unfortunately, a little of his adventurous nature also rubbed off on one of his many pets. Besides the crow, Fred kept a billygoat on a small pasture some way from his home. 'Goat', as he was known to all and sundry, also grew up to develop a tendency to wander and explore the roads of Norfolk, a weakness that invariably got him into trouble.

One of his escapades was related to me, between sudden outbreaks of laughter, by a member of the local police force.

Goat had apparently escaped from the confines of his meadow and decided to seek pastures new in the big outside world. The happy wanderer was eventually spotted some time later quite a considerable distance from home, and through the capable network of the police, Fred was finally traced as his owner. Travelling by police car, Fred came across the delinquent, who was at that moment busily eating his way into a particularly succulent piece of the hedgerow somewhere on the outskirts of Norwich. After Goat had been severely reprimanded and taken into custody, the problem of how to return him to his meadow arose.

A lengthy and heated discussion solved no problems and so, as a last resort, Fred finally opened up the rear door of the Panda patrol car and Goat was ordered inside. Following a great deal of pushing and shoving, not to mention a little encouragement from Fred's boot, Goat was forcefully crammed into the rear seat, much to the chagrin of the police officer. At first bewildered by such strange and unaccustomed goings-on, Goat soon recovered much of his former dignity and began to make the most of the situation, rapidly assuming an air of great self-importance, a luxury the police officer could not hope to retain in view of the prevailing circumstances. The motley crew toured through the busy streets of Norwich, which undoubtedly seemed far busier than usual to the officer of the law, with the 'prisoner', perched proudly in his stately position, doing a spot of window shopping before he was eventually returned to his usual abode.

I also gathered from my informant that Goat was not car trained, and extensive mopping up operations had to be carried out later to the back seat of the vehicle when it returned to base before it was ready to resume rather more orthodox services. Perhaps it was the excitement of the situation that caused Goat to lose some of his self-control; or could it be that he was literally venting his disapproval at being recaptured from his new-found freedom by the long arm of the law?

Goat's activities, alas, after a life befitting the true character he was, were finally curtailed, and he came to a rather sad end. It happened one day when a group of youths with nothing better to do with their spare time decided to have 'a bit of fun'. Poor Goat was stoned and baited relentlessly by the youths and, growing tired of what had developed into a decidedly one-sided battle, he took it into his head to retaliate. Using his only method of defence he soundly butted his antagonists who, no doubt upset by a series of blows to their pride as well as their persons, reported the harmless old beast as being dangerous. Fred was ordered to have the old fellow slaughtered, and so Goat's last journey was to the abbatoir. But his death was not in vain. As I have explained before, Fred was loathe to waste good meat. Besides a few choice joints, Goat's remains were processed into no less than six stone of succulent sausages. When I called on Fred a respectable time after the bereavement, a freshly cured skin adorned his work-room chair to remind him of his old friend. As Fred later remarked, Goat was 'a nice old thing'.

Fred's bubbling enthusiasm for all facets of his work, as I have said before, was highly infectious. It certainly sparked off a new interest for me and I soon began to nurture a desire to learn at least the basic rudiments of the taxidermist's art. With the industriousness of a squirrel gathering together its store of nuts for the coming of winter, I began to acquire some of the funda-mental tools needed for the job. Quite soon I had assembled enough of the necessary equipment to make a start. My admitted-ly crude tool set consisted of a rather rusty penknife sharpened on the concrete path, a pair of small nail scissors (nobody missed those – in fact, I still have them), a packet of borax for preserving the cleaned skins and (collected in an optimistic mood) a varied assortment of needles, pins and thread which I hoped would be used for sewing up and pinning the completed bodies in position – if and when I managed to carry out the earlier stages of the task successfully.

A moorhen was selected as my first victim, easily secured one morning with the rifle along the small drainage channel of a nearby meadow. Plugging both ends with wads of cotton wool to prevent the seepage of unsightly stains, I immediately com-menced the task of parting skin from body. Laying the bird flat on its back and smoothing away the feathers from each side of the breastbone, I made a neat incision from the top of the exposed bone, cutting a shallow line just through the skin along its path until the vent was reached. When opened out the skin parted quite readily from the flesh at first and I began to make good progress, teasing it apart carefully until the leg and wing joints were exposed to halt my advance. These were neatly severed from the body on the inside with the scissors, leaving them firmly joined to the skin which, after cutting carefully through the root of the tail, was turned inside out and rolled up over the neck towards the head. Great care had to be exercised when skinning the head, as I had often watched Fred taking pains to avoid tearing the eyelids or damaging the delicate flaps of skin that were folded neatly into each ear cavity. With infinite and uncharacteristic patience the whole complicated process was accomplished comparativey easily and, removing the now naked body from the empty skin, I congratulated myself on my prowess with the knife. So far – so good. A taxidermist was in the making.

However, when I returned to the next stage of the job it soon became quite apparent that I had merely completed the easiest part of the operation. Worse was to follow – much worse. I was now faced with a sticky, greasy and decidedly bloody skin, which had somehow contrived to become almost half as long again as it had been while still attached to the bird. My problems were obviously only just beginning. Every last trace of blood and grease had to be removed from the inside of the skin before I could even attempt to preserve it and return it to anything like the original shape and form.

After what seemed like hours of patient and careful scraping with the blunt edge of the penknife, the leathery-looking skin appeared to be reasonably clean and ready to receive the coating of preservative. I applied a generous amount of powdered borax, rubbing it well in with my fingers to complete the drying process, and placed this part of my handiwork safely to one side as I contemplated the construction of some form of artificial body to replace the one I had removed. This also proved more difficult than I had imagined but, determined to the end, I managed to build a passable imitation of a skinless moorhen (use your imagination) from a surprisingly large amount of galvanised wire, padded and tightly bound in the necessary places with wood-wool. The end of one length of wire was left jutting out from the front portion of the 'body' and around this I twisted the required amount of cotton wool to represent the bony structure of the neck.

Returning to the skin and setting to work with a stiff mixture of plaster of Paris, I formed what I thought to be a reasonably lifelike shape to represent the head, moulding the putty-like compound to the remains of the precleaned skull bones. The coloured glass eyes, a deep red pair I had managed to persuade Fred to part with, were firmly embedded in the relevant eye sockets and the skin was carefully turned back to its rightful way out. Thus encouraged I placed the artificial body inside the empty skin, passing the wool-bound wire along the narrow neck skin until the skull-bone was pierced, in this way joining the skin and body together. A sharpened wire was inserted, with much difficulty, through the ball of each foot and up along the hollow stem of the legs into the body, and securely fastened by the free end to a heavy board that served as a base. Yet more lengths of sharpened wire were pushed through the thickest portion of both wings to hold them in position against the body. Both edges of the breast incision were carefully sewn up, and a short wire to hold the tail in position completed the finishing touches.

I allowed myself a breather while I stood back to admire my handiwork. What a mess! The head drooped sadly from a sagging neck, the wings hung dejectedly from the stunted frame. Eyes bulging widely, the object had a distinct expression of sheer terror, crouching fearfully as if to conceal itself from imminent doom and displaying evident symptoms of being in the final throes of ornithosis.

Cursing the laws of gravity I attempted a post mortem of my first specimen. What had gone wrong? What had gone right would have been an easier question to answer, and in one word — nothing! The kindest thing would have been to give my reluctant subject a decent burial, but in the end I hardened my heart and decided to keep it as a model against which I could check my rate of progress. I could obviously only improve.

The next endeavour provided little in the form of encouragement. I attempted the preservation of a very handsome tawny owl, a luckily unmarked victim of a car, found dead in a field gateway. During the skinning operation I found to my dismay that the head would not invert; the skull-bone was far too large to pass inside out through the narrow skin of the neck. Following a great number of tentative and patient attempts at the seemingly impossible, I flew into a sudden rage at my incompetence and the owl's lack of elasticity. This is not to be recommended. After a mighty wrench in a do-or-die attitude I ended up with two pieces of useless skin. The owl was a thing of beauty no more.

Back to the drawing board – or to be more precise, back to Fred. It was he who then showed me the correct way of dealing with such obstinate subjects. The proportionately small body is tackled in exactly the same manner as any other bird, but to reach the skull more easily an extra incision can be made in the delicate skin at the back of the head, thereby allowing work to be carried out through the slit, which is sewn up on completion. The same routine applies to the majority of wildfowl and some wading birds; in fact, any subject that has a proportionately large head demands such specialised attention.

I decided to test what I by now felt to be my doubtful and rapidly diminishing skills on a stoat, my very first animal – or to be more truthful, I decided to see if my luck would improve on the previous ornithological failures. I could surely do no worse.

As it was midwinter my usual workshop in the garden shed could not be used, for there was no electric lighting and it was usually dark by the time I returned home from work. The garage was also ruled out in view of the restricted working area and a distinct lack of heating. The kitchen table was certainly out of the question. There was only one place for it – my bedroom upstairs. As skinning stoats in the bedroom would not have been considered a normal practice even in our unusual household, parental consent would not be forthcoming for my request. I would just have to be careful.

Concealing penknife, scissors, file and wood-wool beneath my sweater on the first journey through the kitchen, and wire, plaster of Paris, needles and the body of the deceased on the next, I managed to transfer my main requirements to the bedroom without attracting too much attention. A three-foot square of hardboard proved more difficult to conceal, but when laid out flat on the bed served admirably as a portable workbench. Last but not least I pinched half the toilet roll out of the bathroom, to carry out any necessary mopping up operations on undesirable and telltale blobs of blood and brain tissue. I already had the stoat preserved by Fred to pose as a model, and this I placed on my bedside cabinet for easy reference. At last I was prepared.

Armed only with the blunt penknife, but also with high hopes of emulating my guide and mentor, I proceeded in optimistic ignorance. The actual skinning was carried out with relative ease, although the more delicate parts of the head, eyes and ears proved both tedious and time-consuming. It was only when I began to remove the tail bone that my real problems began. I had often come into contact with the abominably volatile powers of a stoat's scent glands, situated at the root of the tail, and this time was no exception. Though I proceeded with extreme caution the old familiar fragrance suddenly wafted into my nostrils, making my eyes stream with a hitherto unequalled velocity. The stench spread rapidly to saturate the bedroom, and despite throwing the window open it hung heavily on the air in a density that could almost be seen. I rushed to the bathroom with the offending skin, dousing it in a sinkful of cold water and dusting it with a liberal application of talcum powder. Even this had little effect, merely serving to distribute the smell more evenly around the upstairs rooms. At least the pong would be less easily traced to my bedroom, for by the time one reached the top of the staircase one's eyes were already beginning to water! Luckily nobody came to investigate and eventually, by opening all the windows and applying a large amount of sweet smelling talc and after-shave lotion in a few strategic places, the offending smell gradually subsided, allowing me to return to work.

Washing the skin had done nothing to aid my task. The stoat, formerly about 14 inches long from nose to tail, had now acquired some of the characteristics of slack elastic, measuring a full two feet in length and assuming the extended proportions of a furry, snake-like creature. I was almost tempted to chop off the legs; in fact, I briefly toyed with the idea of creating a whole new range of species to add to the animal kingdom, of which I now had the nucleus of a unique collection. Geriatric moorhen, decapitated owls and hairy snakes would no doubt cause quite a stir among the boffins of ornithological and mammalian circles.

Against almost overwhelming odds I pressed on regardless, determined this time at least to finish what I had started. Constructing an artificial body to the same scale as that of the original, I somehow teased and adjusted the elongated pelt and returned it more or less to its former proportions. The result, when sewn up and wired through each leg in turn and fastened to a natural log, was at least more sturdy and rigid than its predecessors, by virtue of the fact that it had four legs instead of two on which to distribute its weight. The body shape was also quite reasonable – legs slightly bent, back arched and tail curled; but the expression on its face, without doubt the most important feature of all, clearly ruined the overall effect of a study in aggression. Using as a guide Fred's model, which bore a characteristic and threatening snarl, I had made an attempt to mould the facial expression along similar lines, curling back the tiny lips to reveal a splendid set of wicked white teeth. My subject would not respond. Try as I might the nearest I could get to the desired aggressive expression was something vaguely resembling a rather silly grin.

In the end I gave up. By that time I had seen quite sufficient of stoats in general and of this awkward and unyielding specimen in particular to last for a very long time. After a few minor adjustments I propped it on the window sill to complete the drying process.

When I awoke next morning the stoat grinned triumphantly back at me from the window ledge. I lay for several minutes trying to figure out just where I had gone wrong and what I could do to improve the wretched creature. It did not look quite as bad as I remembered it from the night before and gradually I began to see it in a different light. Suddenly leaping out of bed I made a few slight adjustments, lifting the tiny blackberry of a nose, pulling forward the long black whiskers and flattening the erect ears. The effect was startling, to say the least. It had suddenly sprung to life. Just how such minor alterations had brought about such a spectacular transformation I was at a loss to explain, but somehow I had done it and succeeded in capturing the desired expression of my subject – quite a boost to a flagging morale.

My triumph was to be short lived. During the following week of unseasonably warm weather the stoat remained proudly displayed on the window sill, threatening to strike at the bluetits that were pinching the putty on the outside of the glass. But not for long. One problem that I was just about to encounter for the first time was that of skin shrinkage during the drying-out period. I soon discovered its undesirable effects, at least in relation to stuffed stoats. My mistakes – and the luckless musteline – reared their equally ugly heads. The ears bent and twisted, the face wrinkled and contorted and the pair of beady eyes gradually began to protrude like those of a King Charles spaniel. When preserving an animal skin shrinkage must be allowed for if one is to avoid the finished article ending up with a distinctly drawn look. This much I now understood. So ended the third lesson. Attempt number three promptly joined its predecessors in the dark recesses of the nearest cupboard.

In keeping with the majority of bad workmen, after exploring all possible excuses for my lack of skill I at last found some consolation in blaming my tools. My implements were undeniably crude and hardly of the standard with which one could be expected to produce a very high degree of craftmanship. I did some research and eventually managed to get in touch with a firm that specialised in surgical supplies, and from them I bought a surgeon's scalpel, a pair of forceps, a brain scoop and a miscellany of other weird and wonderful instruments which looked as if they might come in handy for various skinning, degreasing and construction jobs. The scalpel was an extremely efficient instrument, and I subsequently proved its cutting abilities by removing several neat slices from the index finger of my left hand when skinning a pheasant.

It was first put to less painful use in skinning a large female coypu, one of those huge, fearsome-looking (and luckily mainly vegetarian) rodents which at that time frequented the river meadows and Broads of Norfolk in alarming profusion, having multiplied rapidly following the escape of a few individuals from various fur farms where their thick pelts were produced to supply nutria for the fur trade. Nutria was a fashionable fur for quite some time, but I rather suspect that few fashionable women would be quite so keen to wear it if they were to encounter the coat's previous owner. Not that I had any intentions of making a coat, for such a formidable task would require a considerable amount of time, skill and very hard work, not to mention a large number of dead coypus. However, I had always rather fancied a fur hat and, after 'acquiring' a huge sow coypu from a ministry trap on the river bank, I took rough head measurements and designed a hat that could be completed from a single pelt.

Having skinned the animal (and the ball of my left thumb), I proceeded with the awesome task of preserving the hide. Borax and elbow grease in equally large amounts gave a reasonably light and supple finish, and, after cutting and sewing, the hat gradually took shape. It was very warm and comfortable to wear, although the completed article retained a rather unpleasant odour that was particularly noticeable in warm weather. At times it became advisable to stand on the downwind side when in conversation to avert a telltale wrinkling of nostrils, and to avoid embarrassment when entering a confined space it was necessary to remove my hat. When paying house calls I normally dropped it outside in the fresh air, but one such occasion proved to be the undoing of my headgear. Calling on my cousin John one evening, I dropped my hat on the conservatory floor against the back door. It was quickly discovered and set upon by John's Jack Russell bitch, which, obviously thinking she had discovered an over-grown rat in John's conservatory and having been trained to seek out and dispose of its less formidable cousins, repeatedly shook and bit it in the accustomed manner, much to the amusement of all concerned. By the time I arrived on the scene there was very little left except a bundle of tattered skin and a few remnants of the lining.

With my new tools and after much trial and error I began at last to achieve some measure of competence in the taxidermy field, with much credit going to Fred, who took great pains to encourage his ham-fisted pupil. My work improved to such a degree that very soon I began receiving enquiries from potential customers. When I could find the time I accepted, only too glad of the chance of gaining experience. My fees were small, as I charged according to the overall results of each specimen sold, but nevertheless I soon made enough cash to keep me supplied with scalpel blades, sticking plaster and finger bandages, all of which were in constant demand.

One of the more common though less skilful jobs was the cleaning and setting up of skulls, most of which had to be lightly parboiled until the flesh could be scraped away, then bleached clean and white. The cleaning process was quite easy when the skulls were small and in a fresh condition and could be boiled in a saucepan kept specially for the job, but more often than not those received were large, partly decomposed and very evil smelling. Following several complaints about the unhygienic state of the kitchen cooker it became necessary to resort to a large, electric copper boiler, which could be used in the fresh air of the garden. Even then I could not accommodate the bigger trophies, and these had to be buried underground to allow the fleshy parts to decompose by a more natural but far longer process. This method was quite acceptable, provided of course that I kept a careful record of when and where each specimen was laid to rest. As proof of my occasional lapses in the matter, I still encounter long forgotten remains at various points around the garden, by either falling headlong over a protruding antler, blunting the lawn mower blades on a tough skull-bone or watching spellbound as the dog exhumes yet another strange and smelly object buried long ago in the vegetable patch.

It was during my early days in the taxidermy field that I began to get somewhat sidetracked and to take an interest in one of the oldest of all field sports, one that had scarcely attracted my attention before. The ancient art of courting, I suppose, should not properly be included under the admittedly extensive label of field sports, but then, as the field was the very place where the majority of my education in the art took place, perhaps it can just be squeezed into the category. Unfortunately, few girls appeared to have a real interest in spending a freezing night waiting for the geese to flight under a full December moon, no matter how romantic, or, for that matter, any great desire to take a turn on the rabbiting spade when attempting to retrieve a laid-up ferret.

Similarly, at the time I could summon up little interest in the rowdy discotheques, dances and pop stars of which my early female companions were so fond, for how could the wailing groups compare with the liquid notes of a nightingale pouring forth from the copse on a summer's night, or the exciting treble bark of a dog fox wooing his chosen partner in the winter moonlight? But feeling the need for, amongst other things, female companionship, I set out on the longest and most difficult hunting expedition of my life. During the following year I achieved but one thing; I found the old adage 'True love never runs smoothly' to be quite accurate.

One particular old boy, who on his own admittance had been a bit of a lad in his younger days, proffered some earthy advice.

'Me boy,' he said, twinkle in his eye, 'It's like riding a bicycle – any bike's good enough to learn on, but once you've learnt, get a good one!'

My deep involvement in country pursuits ended many an encounter. I had been dating a girl in the nearby town and as she had suffered my rather scant attentions for at least a month we were 'going steady'. However, things were soon to become decidedly unsteady, as more often than not I would be out with the gun most summer evenings, and on each successive night always seemed to arrive a few minutes later. This rather sorry state of affairs continued for quite some time, until one night when I skidded to a stop outside her house at least an hour late, arriving at top speed in a scream of smoking tyres. The oft-used and too familiar excuse of mechanical trouble failed to dispel her anger – even though I had taken the precaution of smearing my hands with grease – especially when she caught a strong whiff of gunpowder from the twelve-bore left carelessly on the back seat; and insult was added to injury by a couple of fresh rabbits discovered hidden under my shooting jacket. Then came the by now well-known ultimatum. I was informed in no uncertain manner that I had to choose between the untold pleasures of her company and 'that gun'. There were, she added, plenty more fish in the sea. Fish! There were plenty more of those in the river too and, as I pointed out, very few of them ever answered back. Thus we parted and went our separate ways, she to her 'fishing' and I to my rod and line.

A few months later I began dating a girl I had known for a number of years, who lived in the village and worked locally at a wildlife park. She had attracted my attention by presenting me with a pair of feet from a dead eagle owl, which immediately gained her good marks, and our shared interest in wildlife at once put us on a firm basis. In due course Barbara began to accompany me on some of my sporting forays and country pursuits. To cut a long story short, during a very extensive courtship Barbara was put through a gruelling course of shooting, fishing, taxidermy and a wide range of other country sports, all of which she passed with flying colours. She was a good all-rounder in the shooting field. A splendid flusher of game, she would enter even the thickest of cover without qualm, kept reasonably still and quiet when in the confines of a pigeon hide and became a dab hand at retrieving and dispatching shot game. As a form of dowry I was frequently presented with miscellaneous birds and beasts for my taxidermy collection from the wildlife park where she was employed. What more could the budding shooter/fisherman/taxidermist/falconer hope for?

Barbara accompanied me on my visits to see Fred, with whom she immediately struck up a friendship. She was more literally struck by Crow, for as we fought our way through a mass of completed work to reach Fred's workbench, she noticed Crow standing quietly and in his most alluring attitude at the front of his cage. Fred was slow to issue his usual warning about his feathered friend.

'Watch he doesn't . . .'

'Ouch!'

Too late: Crow had deftly removed a neat chunk from Barbara's lower lip before triumphantly retreating to the rear of his cage, evidently delighted to make the acquaintance of such an easy victim and mentally carving another notch on his perching bar. Having worked for a number of years with wildlife, however, Barbara had already accumulated a number of scars from various encounters with otters, wildcats, foxes and the odd lynx or wolf. The mere peck of a carrion crow, despite a profusely bleeding lip, was dismissed as comparatively insignificant and she was soon encouraging the old bird to show off his remarkable range of party tricks. Crow's enjoyable evening was marred only by the fact that Barbara kept well clear of his stabbing beak as we squeezed past on our way out.

As Barbara was obviously acceptable to all concerned, in due course we managed to buy a piece of building land within catapult range of where I was born and raised, and began the mammoth task of erecting a roof over our heads. With this completed – or at least habitable – we finally decided to get married. Never ones to stand on ceremony, we made arrangements for a brief and secret visit to the local registry office to obtain the blessing of the Registrar and the necessary paperwork required for such a venture. Not being too well versed in such matters I gladly entrusted Barbara with the task of attending to the formalities and fixing a date at the registry office. By some strange quirk of fate the date finally arranged coincided with the opening day of the wildfowling season and plans had already been made by the local farmers for a combined assault on the ever-increasing population of Canada geese, which were causing considerable crop damage in the area. The first of September was one event not to be missed. I resolved to keep both appointments.

Feigning toothache as an excuse for my leaving work early we eventually set out, with me holding my jaw in apparent mortal agony and Barbara looking suitably sympathetic in view of my distress. First call was at the jewellers. Choosing a ring presented more difficulties than anticipated and very soon I had begun to wish that I had gone to the dentist's, as its purchase began to look as though it would turn out to be a rather painful experience. The only ring that filled our requirements of being both pleasing to the eye and not too hard on the wallet was much too large. The saleswoman tried her best to be helpful.

'It can always be made smaller', she said. 'The alteration could be completed in less than a week. When would you be needing it?'

'In about five minutes', replied Barbara, consulting her watch. 'I'll bring it back later!'

With Barbara clutching our purchase and me clutching the remains of my wallet we arrived at the other end of the town with a couple of minutes to spare before the ceremony was due to take place. Sitting together in the empty waiting room had, in fact, a marked similarity to waiting at the dentist's to have a tooth extracted; that unpleasant stomach-churning feeling of nervous anticipation. In due course a face beamed round the door.

'Is everyone here?' enquired the Registrar, whose facial expression dropped visibly when he viewed the empty room. We confirmed that 'everyone' was indeed present, glancing sideways at each other as proof of the fact.

'But where are your witnesses?' the face continued.

Witnesses?

'Well . . . er . . . er . . . we thought perhaps you supplied those', I stammered, not having had the slightest idea that we needed such a thing.

With an audible sigh the Registrar left us to study the claustrophobic little office, but after a time-consuming search that apparently encompassed the entire building he returned triumphant, leading a giggling shorthand typist and a junior office boy.

Within minutes the brief and relatively painless ceremony was completed and we set out in haste to fulfil my second appointment. Stopping briefly en route to pick up my gun and the necessary equipment, I arrived at the marsh just in time for the first flight of the new season. To some, wildfowl may seem a rather unusual quarry to pursue on one's wedding night, when I should have perhaps forsaken the geese for less elusive quarry; but don't forget, it had been a full seven months since I had last viewed a goose along the barrels of a twelve-bore. Be warned — goose fever is strong indeed.

7

A Hunting Bird

I became aware of a mounting trepidation as I steered the van from the main road and bumped noisily along a deserted country lane to where, at the bottom of an undulating hillside, a large red brick house nestled cosily among a gathering of tall oaks and beeches surrounded by emerald post-and-rail fenced cattle pastures. There appeared to be good reason for my apprehension. My hawking apprenticeship, carried out on a motley collection of kestrels – mostly injured waifs and strays – was about to be rewarded; the hitherto fruitless search for a real hunting bird had finally paid off. I was soon to become the proud, though slightly nervous, owner of a large female goshawk. I knew little of this particular bird, other than that she had been trained and flown for the duration of a winter season, but would now need to be rested during the summer moult and intensively retrained before she could be flown at quarry again in the autumn.

The phone call of the previous evening had sounded rather ominous, being the main cause of the swarm of butterflies that were fluttering wildly around my stomach.

'She's a bit . . . a bit . . . er . . . spiteful,' I was reluctantly informed regarding the hawk. 'I feel it's only fair to warn you, she's already had her previous owner.'

In her keenness while being flown the hawk had somehow mistaken the ungloved hand of her trainer for a lost rabbit and, eager not to let it escape, had vigorously and savagely 'killed' it in the accustomed manner, a painful process lasting the best part of half an hour until the human quarry had stopped struggling and finally conceded defeat. Needless to say, a description of the subsequent hospitalisation of the falconer did little to allay my fears and I must confess to not sleeping too well during the night, waking repeatedly in a succession of cold sweats as I anticipated the morrow.

I drew up with the van as though in a dream, knees trembling uncontrollably and heart threatening at any moment to burst through my rib cage. I must admit to being a coward as regards pain. I had come prepared for the worst, literally armed with a huge eagle gauntlet that protected almost to the elbow, and the rest of my upper anatomy was heavily padded with two thick sweaters and a jacket. On the passenger seat beside me lay a wire-mesh fencing mask that had already seen more dangerous service in training a golden eagle. When fully clad it was imposs-ible to determine by my appearance whether I was about to tackle a swarm of angry bees or act as a stand-in burglar for a police dog training session. It looked highly unlikely that I was about to embark on another chapter in the gentle art of hawking.

I was agreeably surprised – though somewhat humbled – to find my charge poised quietly on a ring perch at the rear of the house, still as a statue and looking the very picture of good-natured calmness. Venom was a large female goshawk. She seemed immense when compared to a kestrel, weighing on the heavy side of three pounds and boasting an extending wingspan of almost four feet. She looked ready and capable of tackling anything – me included. Her gentle unblinking eyes, already turning a warm shade of amber with age, hid her true disposition, for as I later discovered they could in a flash transform to a fierce glaring red when something disturbed or displeased her and a sudden display of temper was imminent. The most striking part of her anatomy – quite literally – was a pair of colossal yellow feet tipped with three-quarter-inch spikes, and if the grip of a kestrel was mildly painful, Venom's could only be described with one word – paralysing. During one of her not infrequent bad moods she would crouch menacingly on the glove, eyes afire like miniature red-hot coals and feet mutilating the glove in strong convulsions, a practice which, even through the strong leather gauntlet, could be almost guaranteed to bring the tears to one's eyes.

The journey home was far less hazardous than I had expected

and Venom was soon safely installed in the converted garden shed that was to be her mews, where she would be fed and tended all summer long while I dreamed of the day when I would take her up for training to catch quarry. At present she had to be gorged to repletion during the summer moult to ensure that the new set of wing and tail feathers would grow healthy and strong, allowing her the full potential of her flying powers. She could not be flown for the duration of the moult, as the reduction in food necessary to make a hawk keen enough to fly at quarry and to return to her trainer for a reward of food would have upset the balance of diet needed to promote good feather growth.

Summer eventually passed into autumn and at long last she was ready. She was hard penned – that is, the final flight feather had reached its fullest extent and had drained of blood – and ready for training to begin.

I shall not attempt to describe the complicated rigmarole of training a hunting bird in great detail, as there are others far more competent than I to explain such a delicate process. Very briefly the general idea is as follows. The wild hawk is, by gentleness, inducement and reward, encouraged to accustom itself to the falconer and learn to accept its every meal on the falconer's gloved fist, thereby discovering the glove to be a desirable and rewarding place to be. When it will allow itself to be fed and carried without fear of the falconer it is said to have become manned to the glove, from which it is then gradually introduced to other sights and sounds all alien to a wild hawk. Dogs, cars, machines, cattle and other equally terrifying objects all have to be carefully introduced and accepted before the hawk is fully manned and the training proper can begin.

Accepting the glove as its regular feeding place, the hawk is then encouraged to fly on a line, or creance, over gradually increasing distances for its daily meals, which it duly receives as a reward for each flight to the glove, thereby gradually learning to return to the falconer, who calls or whistles the hawk when a reward is in the offing. When the bird will fly to the glove immediately when called over long distances, the creance is finally removed and it is allowed to fly completely free. It is then time to go in search of quarry.

Venom was, and to a certain extent remained, a rather wild

hawk. Her reactions during training were, to put it mildly, unpredictable. One day she would be absolutely terrified of a particular person or object, stubbornly refusing to remain on the glove in its presence and instead hanging upside down by her leather jesses, despite constant attempts to restore her to a vertical position. The puzzling thing was that the very next day she could often face an identical situation with complete indifference, standing contentedly on my fist, one leg tucked up into her barred flank, to all appearances without a care in the world.

During the latter stages of Venom's training she occasionally showed reluctance to return directly to the glove, so, as an alternative means of retrieving her from miscellaneous unclimbable trees, the tops of the telegraph poles, house roofs and other equally inaccessible perching places, I found it necessary to introduce her to the lure. A lure is fashioned to represent roughly a bird or animal the hawk recognises as food, and any bird declining the offer of the glove can usually be tempted down to the more natural sight of a moving lure, providing of course that it has been thoroughly taught that the lure holds food.

I made an effective working model from a small horseshoe scrounged from the blacksmith, bound well with a cushion of twine and covered with a skin of supple leather. A pair of mallard wings were fastened to the shoe with a strong leather bootlace, leaving both ends free for attaching the garnish of meat. The contraption proved most effective for taking her up following an abortive flight, when she would invariably perch in the nearest tree to wait for her lost quarry to reappear below. If all attempts to eject her prospective dinner from its hiding place failed, the lure could be produced and dragged along the ground beneath her, being twitched in the required lifelike manner from long range by a length of cord. Following a brief contemplation she would usually swoop from the tree to seize it, and after consuming the small portion of meat it held could be taken back on the glove with relative ease from her simulated kill.

Apart from a few minor setbacks Venom's training progressed quite smoothly. Her main aversion was an intense dislike of almost 99 per cent of the human race, the mere glimpse of a stranger on the far horizon being sufficient to send her into a vicious fit of flapping and screaming. Quite understandably the majority of people encountered in the neighbouring village seemed unable at first to accept the sight of a large hawk with indifference, which only made things worse, but as we became a regular and familiar sight we were gradually accepted as part of the everyday scene. There were of course several annoying and unfortunate meetings with people on our daily walks, and the height of indignity came one evening while strolling quietly along the village street, when a battered estate car slowed down beside us and a row of young heads emerged from the open window to gaze in rapt attention at such an unusual sight.

'Look, Mum, he's got a pigeon on a string', one of the little brats expounded gleefully, not being too strong on his ornithological studies.

'Are you going to let it go, mister?' another chimed in.

'Oh look, it's fallen off. Poor thing!'

Venom, overcome by their noisy and unwarranted inquisitiveness, had chosen that very moment to launch herself from the glove in a fit of fright and temper, dangling upside down by her jesses and emitting a series of earsplitting screams while at the same time attempting to dislocate my shoulder by her bating. Grunting noncommitally, I continued walking and was filled with great relief as the vehicle accelerated noisily away, the row of heads transferring as one to the rear window to the accompaniment of a succession of 'ohs' and 'ahs' until the car was, thankfully, out of sight.

Venom's speed and flying expertise soon improved with practice. She had shed her summer store of excess fat and her training schedule had gone more or less to plan. She returned fast and hard when recalled for food while fastened on the creance. It was almost time to take her in search of a kill. I decided that the first attempt would be at a moorhen. Being comparatively slow and awkward in the air, a moorhen would undoubtedly offer the best possible chance of success despite the added weight and drag of the creance to impede Venom's flight.

The big day arrived and, checking Venom's weight carefully, I tied the creance through the looped ends of her jesses, my fingers all thumbs and shaking uncontrollably with mounting anticipation of the day ahead. I removed the brass swivel to cut the weight of her load, for the creance would inevitably drag along the ground as she flew, holding her back and braking the speed of flight considerably. At this advanced stage of training the creance is normally removed and the hawk flown free before its introduction to quarry, but with Venom I wanted to make really sure of her reactions and keenness when confronted with a possible kill.

The plan of action was to approach slowly and, if Venom's legs bells allowed, quietly to one of the small ponds on the largest of our meadows, which always held a moorhen or two during the daylight hours. With any luck, those dabbling in the shallows would run to hide in the rushes at the water's edge, from where they could be flushed at a reasonably comfortable range to give Venom every possible chance of an easy capture.

As we entered the meadow through a slender gap in the boundary blackthorn scrub, a redshank, ever watchful in its assumed role of marsh warden, lifted daintily from a patch of oozing mud to trill protestingly above its province, warning all and sundry of our presence on the marsh. The call was taken up by the resident flock of Canada geese, whose bugle-like calls echoed eerily in the distant woods as they craned their necks bolt upright to follow our movements. So much for our silent approach. The single croaking note of a moorhen drifted a hundred yards on the faint breeze towards us. The pond had not let us down. As we stealthily approached across the green sward two birds scuttled across its surface, cutting a path through the green slime of algae and diving for cover at the far end in a thicket of withered sedge. The quarry was marked to ground!

With all haste we reached the spot and I began probing

excitedly among the tightly woven sedge, searching methodically for signs of its hiding place. Wide footmarks were imprinted clearly in the dark mud beside a vole run, leading into a small opening among the largest clump of rushes. I parted the dense cover carefully, revealing a moorhen squatting low, quite still and unperturbed as it waited for us to pass. With a final adjustment to the creance I held Venom high above the bird ready for the slip and then, barely able to contain myself, probed it from cover with a long stick.

The moorhen splashed out awkwardly squawking in alarm, to fly rapidly away across the surface of the shallow pond, skidding around sharply to make good its escape in a nearby blackthorn clump, from where it gave vent to a series of decidedly seductive clucks. Venom had scarcely moved! She appeared totally uninterested. Doubting the evidence of my own eyes I hunted frantically for the remaining bird, which had finally come to rest beneath the undermined bank where its plumage blended effectively with the dark mud. This one even refused to take the unnecessary precaution of launching into the air, for its spindly green legs carried it quickly to the safety of the hedge bottom, where it promptly joined its colleague, rejoicing gleefully in a double chorus at the pointlessness of our combined efforts to catch them.

This was a totally unforeseen setback. Just as everything had seemed to be going so well and our goal was in sight, Venom had failed to respond in the expected manner, and my hopes and aspirations plummeted to an all-time low. What was wrong? I could only assume that she had failed to recognise the moorhen as a possible source of food, and with this in mind I went out later armed with a four-ten to hunt the overgrown river banks, eventually returning with a single moorhen, dropped into the river with the little gun. Instead of cutting the bird up as normal when feeding I fastened a short length of cord to its legs and, placing Venom on a garden fence post, dragged the moorhen along the ground in front of her, jerking and twitching it repeatedly in a lifelike manner.

Suddenly, her natural instincts at last awakening, she sprang and struck, taking the bird squarely across the back with both feet. I continued to tug on the cord as she sat astride the moorhen, and at each movement she gripped harder and with more determination. She soon began to tear beakfuls of black feathers from its breast, tossing them aside with gay abandon in an effort to reach the body. Ignoring the thick layer of fluffy down she broke through the leathery skin and tore warm flesh from the breast, devouring it in great, greedy chunks as if she had not eaten for a week.

I allowed her to take her fill, and by the time her appetite was fully dulled all that remained of the moorhen was a few of the larger bones, a wormlike mass of green intestines and the pile of black feathers. The rest, feet included, was tightly packed into her bulging crop, which had assumed the size of a cricket ball and had blown up out of all proportion to the rest of her body. She even appeared to have some difficulty in holding herself upright on the perch, so heavy was her load. After this gorge it would obviously be quite some time before she would be in condition for flying again, but I hoped by then she would have learned how to recognise and deal with the next moorhen she encountered on the marsh.

On the following day Venom was allowed no food. She spent most of the day on a ring perch in a shaded corner of the weathering ground, amusing herself by plucking the fur from a rabbit's foot. When the comparative cool of the evening descended she was beginning to display signs of hunger again, screaming loudly whenever I appeared in sight, obviously expecting a late meal. A cock blackbird, searching for its supper among the trimmed grass of the lawn, came bouncing past a few feet from where she stood. She watched its every movement carefully as it toyed with a piece of rabbit fur and suddenly, unable to contain herself any longer, bated at it wildly to the extent of her leash. The blackbird scuttled away in alarm to alight on the mews roof above her, scolding angrily from its vantage point. Venom turned to face it again, wings arched, threatening to bate again until it flew, still chattering loudly, out of the garden. This was indeed a welcome change. I had never seen her show such aggression towards another bird before and I could hardly wait for the morrow, when she would be in peak condition for flying again.

Saturday morning dawned bright and calm, with just the

faintest hint of a westerly breeze on the already warm air. A few late swallows were on the wing against feathery puffs of cumulus floating among the light blue of the early sky, perfect conditions for a hawking foray. As I carried Venom to the marshes she displayed obvious signs of keenness, bating hard at a blackbird as it crossed our path from the tangles of a blackberry patch. I held her back, knowing full well that the blackbird would easily outwit her among the dense jungle of the hedgerow.

We began by hunting the marsh perimeter, where a deep drainage channel carried excess water from the surrounding fields, seeing nothing at which to attempt a flight. Several of the smaller marsh denizens were disturbed from patches of withering rushes; reed buntings, meadow pipits and a handful of snipe probing holes along the muddy banks. Each time a snipe exploded from under my feet I could feel Venom tense her whole body in readiness for flight. She was really keen at last. Of moorhen there was not a sign, not even a telltale ripple at the water's edge to betray their presence, but as we neared the centre of the marsh I caught a brief glimpse of one as it sped to a small clump of interwoven sedges and willow roots 60 yards ahead. Venom had seen it race for cover and watched expectantly as we approached, bells tinkling as she shifted impatiently on the glove, anticipating the chase.

The yellowing sedges were sparse, offering little in the form of protection or concealment, and at the base of a willow stump a small black and white tail protruded just above the water level of a little pool, its body wedged firmly into a crevice among the twisting roots. I tapped gently beside it. The tail turned slowly. Suddenly the moorhen burst from hiding, churning the muddy water into the consistency of thick oxtail soup in an ungainly attempt to get airborne. Venom was slow to follow. Bewildered by the frantic splashing she had allowed the bird to clear the water before giving chase. These vital few seconds had given the moorhen a good advantage and it made a bee-line for a clump of brambles with Venom still a good ten yards behind. Gaining sanctuary, it hurled itself among the prickly briars and Venom, luckily deciding not to follow, flew up into a tall willow directly above, to perch swaying precariously on a slender bough and contemplate the moorhen's rapid disappearance.

What was I to do now? Should I call her back to the fist before attempting to flush the moorhen again, or leave her at her vantage point in the tree where she could get a bird's eye view of any movement below, possibly allowing her the advantage of a good start? I decided to leave her in the tree, hoping desperately that the creance would not tangle among the twisted branches if and when she resumed the chase.

I searched the cover thoroughly, but several minutes had elapsed before the moorhen reappeared, flapping noisily from the far edge of the trailing thorns. The jangle of hawk bells drowned the flapping of wings as Venom swooped in a long glide to give chase. The creance snaked free of the willow and the chase was on! Both birds gained height above the grass with Venom closing the gap as they raced across the meadow. The gap decreased – ten yards – five yards – two – and suddenly the moorhen upended in the sky, clenched in the grip of Venom's talons. She parachuted heavily to earth with the unaccustomed burden, landing clumsily in an undignified heap where, after a short tussle, she stood, wings mantled possessively, claiming her first kill.

At last! After all the hours of careful and patient training, mile upon endless mile of walking, days of manning and flying to the fist, we had actually experienced a successful flight. Even if we had no more, all the hard and time-consuming work of the preceding weeks would somehow still seem very worthwhile. As I watched her gorging the reward of our labours I was filled with an almost overwhelming sense of achievement and satisfaction, the like of which I had seldom experienced before.

Even after such an encouraging performance, however, a small cloud still hung ominously on our horizon. Venom's training was as yet incomplete. The time was fast approaching when she must be flown free. It was a few more days before I hardened my heart sufficiently to take the risk of the first free flight, but I finally ran out of convenient excuses to delay the ordeal further. The great moment of truth had at last arrived.

That afternoon, with trembling hands, I removed the leash and swivel, twisting the jesses tightly to avoid the loops snagging on any branches or undergrowth if Venom should give chase to quarry. My mind flashed back vividly to the time of my lost kestrel as I again searched the small meadow for a moorhen, for moorhen it must surely be to give her the best possible chance of a kill with which she would remain after the flight. A missed flight could result in her raking away to who knew where, possibly to sit and sulk in a distant tree well out of my sight. As we methodically searched the meadows back and forth along the overgrown ditches, I noticed a dark shape scuttle into a thistle bed from the open ground — a moorhen for certain.

Approaching the tangled growth I placed myself between the clump of dead thistle stems and an adjacent drain, thus hoping to cut off the bird's expected path of escape. I worked noisily into the clump, beating the dry withered stems as I moved forward. Suddenly and without the least warning a beautiful cock pheasant, resplendent in his chain mail plumage of old age, exploded from our path. At the same instant that he broke cover Venom shot off like an arrow in his wake. What had I done? As hunter and quarry veered sharply around to clear the deep ditch I instantly regretted releasing her at such a strong and cunning quarry — and on her first free flight! But by then it was too late. She was on her own, leaving me, completely helpless, to stand and watch the outcome.

The cock climbed steeply in a vain attempt to clear the elms of the bordering hedge but then, noting the speed of his pursuer, dropped to cover in his bid for escape. Venom followed relentlessly, plunging boldly into the waist-high bracken beneath the golden elms, severing all contact between us save the urgent tinkling of her leg bells. She meant to have this one. A noisy combat followed as she presumably made contact among the vegetation, but soon all was ominously quiet until the sound of drumming wings reached my ears. Had she got it, or was the flapping from the pheasant making good its escape?

Seeing neither sight nor sound of either bird I was by this time extremely agitated. The only possible way of reaching the spot was by crossing a rough bridge of railway sleepers well upstream. The drain was far too wide to jump and its bed consisted almost solely of thick, glutinous and almost bottomless mud. Cursing myself for such stupidity I ran the 200 yards to the bridge in record time, crossed the wooden baulks and raced back along the opposite bank, my passage hampered by a clinging, interwoven, infernal jungle of twisted bracken and nettles. Arriving at last completely out of breath I searched frantically among the dense forest of bracken and willowherb into which the pair had disappeared.

At last a bell tinkled close by — behind the next clump of bracken? I parted the crackling fronds carefully to reveal an unforgettable sight. It was almost magical. Venom was standing proudly over the dead pheasant, one yellow talon grasping his scarlet wattled head and the other foot clamped squarely across his back. The immaculate plumage of the old cock reflected the last rays of the setting sun and his huge tail was fanned wide, almost blending with the backcloth of bracken on which the bird sprawled. Venom crouched possessively as I praised her, spreading her wings wide over the motionless body surrounded by a handful of burnished copper feathers. I was floating on air. Venom had taken her first pheasant in fine style.

Now that Venom had quite literally earned her wings, my purpose was to use her as frequently as time would allow in the pursuit of our real objective, the taking of wild game. With the advent of autumn the dwindling areas of thick foliage opened up new places for us to explore and the search for game was much simplified by the decrease in cover. Hunting the fields, woods and marshes daily, our bag consisted almost solely of moorhen, although the majority were becoming surprisingly adept in the combined arts of self-preservation and concealment. Moorhen flushed over open ground rarely offered the chance of a testing flight, but amongst thick cover they were a vastly different kettle of fish. Here, as in water, they were in their element and the odds were often heavily stacked in their favour. The apparently ungainly birds could twist and turn in the undergrowth with surprising agility, and on more than one occasion a black and white stubby tail was seen rapidly vanishing into the depths of a rabbit burrow.

I searched for other game. Rabbits, so prolific on the warm summer evenings during our training sessions, were now in short supply owing to a local outbreak of myxomatosis. Those that survived the virus rarely left the safety of their burrows except at dusk, when it was far too risky to fly a hawk in the failing light. Myxomatosis had taken its cruel and heavy toll throughout most of the small warrens on the farm and many previously well-tenanted burrows were now standing empty, a delicate lacework of spiders' webs barring the front doors. Venom seldom encountered a rabbit, except on the occasions that we came across one of the remaining disease-ridden animals, a pitiful shadow of its former self, eyes swollen out of all proportion to the rest of its emaciated body, wandering aimlessly and suffering dreadfully in the last stages of the foul man-made plague. There was little pleasure or excitement to be gained from such a one-sided contest as the rabbits provided, but nonetheless it was all good experience for Venom, and above all it saved the stricken animals from many days of suffering.

On the rare occasions that Venom flew a strong and healthy rabbit, success was rare. Although she would chase and sometimes come to grips with the rabbit, she usually grabbed it by the rear end and was more often than not kicked off in an extremely undignified heap. Judging by the looks I received at such times I was evidently to blame for her lack of success. Woe betide any hand that was not protected by a thick gauntlet when picking her up afterwards.

But whatever the shortcomings of Venom's skills, she certainly made up for them in keenness and character. Her eagerness to pursue virtually anything that moved became something of a nuisance at times, as she often bated at any small bird or beast that just happened to cross our path, her bells ringing loudly to warn other larger and more desirable game of our approach. Her complete indifference as to what constituted legitimate prey for a goshawk would no doubt be frowned upon in the higher realms of falconry, but it ensured that for us no outing was ever dull or repetitive. Often we returned from a full afternoon's hunting with only a rat, mouse or hedge sparrow to show for our efforts, but certainly it was all good fun.

One afternoon, following a downpour of warm rain, we were hunting a small, triangular patch of sedgy marshland not far from the river's edge. Venom bated repeatedly towards an open area of short grass, apparently attracted by some kind of prey in hiding. I scanned the area thoroughly from a distance of a few yards, seeing absolutely nothing that could have been the cause of her excitement. As she was very insistent, and I expected her prey to be a mouse in hiding, I released Venom at the next bate. She dived to the ground and snatched gingerly with an extended foot, but then leapt up again in the manner of the proverbial cat on hot bricks. After she had completed two more dives in quick succession I reached the spot and saw the reason for her unusual behaviour – a frog!

The large, slimy, green frog, no doubt bewildered by such strange goings-on and distressed by such a fierce and unprovoked attack, jumped high in the air, taking a large leap in the general direction of the nearest drain where it would be safe from the undesirable attentions of this annoying raptor. Venom struck again as it hit the ground, apparently taking the unfortunate amphibian in both talons. But no, the frog leapt once more, leaving the puzzled hawk crouching at the spot it had so recently vacated. Its next gigantic leap brought it to within easy reach of the drain and with a final resounding plop it splashed into the murky green depths, sinking rapidly to the bottom where it lay conspicuously outlined against the dark mud. Venom stood on a tuft of grass on the bank, head cocked quizzically on one side as she peered in disbelief beneath the widening ripples at the strange creature that had managed to evade her so easily. Frog was definitely off the menu that afternoon.

It was following another abortive flight that Venom made one

of her more unusual captures. She had tried a full-grown rabbit flushed at long range from a tall wheat stubble but, being rather too close to its warren to offer a good chance, the rabbit popped into the nearest burrow after Venom's half-hearted stoop. Not to be outdone she climbed to alight in a leafy oak, half-way up on a rotting limb that jutted out over the field. She searched below for the elusive coney and, when it failed to reappear, settled herself for a long vigil until the rabbit or something equally desirable happened to come along. I stood patiently below her, 15 yards upwind, calling, whistling, throwing the lure and generally making a fool of myself. For all the good it did I might just as well have called the lapwings gyrating overhead to come to hand. She was quite happy in the tree, from where she could absorb a pleasant and uninterrupted view of the surrounding fields. It was made abundantly clear that she would return to my fist only when it pleased her to do so, and not before.

And then it happened. She suddenly stiffened. The leg drawn into her long barred flank feathers was now aiding her balance as she leaned forward on her lofty perch, poised to fly. She was not showing even the remotest interest in me or anything I had to offer, as her gaze seemed to be focused on a point way above my head, somewhere across the open field. I still saw no movement of prey as Venom slipped soundlessly from the oak on closed wings, straightening to an even keel just above ground level. She flew very low, her flickering wing tips almost brushing the stubble as she beat steadily past me, totally absorbed by her target. She must have spotted another rabbit squatting in the stubble.

Venom had covered at least 60 yards across the field when she suddenly struck. No noise, no signs of a struggle, just a quick darting snatch as she reached the chosen spot. She had evidently caught something, for her head was bent low, peering between her feet, which were hidden from my view by the tall corn stubble. What had she taken this time? I ran to see.

A reputedly fierce, mighty, female goshawk of almost three pounds looks a trifle silly mantling possessively over a dead skylark. As I said at the beginning of this chapter, though, Venom was always unpredictable.

8

Doggy Mixture

While I was engrossed in the pleasure and interest of hunting almost every day with Venom, another training project was in full swing. My wife Barbara, who had undertaken the mammoth task of educating our newly acquired German shorthaired pointer bitch for use in the hawking field, was at last beginning to make some progress. I have never had much success with training a working dog, largely due to my own incompetence and lack of patience, and was therefore quite relieved when Barbara volunteered her services as unpaid dog handler. I had undoubtedly started out on the wrong foot – or to be more specific, on the wrong animal.

Pixie, our large, fat, lazy black and white cat of childhood days, at first displayed little interest in my early hunting exploits, wisely fearing for her safety besides doubting my skill in providing her with a bonus meal with the catapult. The merest twang of catapult elastic was sufficient to send her scuttling for refuge behind one of the large tubs in the mealshed. The air rifle, however, aroused in her rather more than a cursory interest – not, I might add, through any sense of obligation to me, but more as a means of satisfying her gargantuan appetite for dead sparrows.

So Pixie became my constant companion, acting in the position of a somewhat scaled-down retriever. Whether it was a silent vigil within range of a well-used rat hole, stalking sparrows in the orchard or a more optimistic foray further afield in search of larger quarry, each time I ventured out with the gun under my arm the cat would tag along, trailing silently behind at a

III

respectable five yards. As I walked, she walked. If I stopped, the cat did likewise, duplicating my movements like a remotely controlled shadow.

Pixie seemed to possess an extremely well-developed sixth sense. She displayed an uncanny knack of knowing whether or not a shot had been successful. If the bullet passed wide of a potential victim she remained the customary five yards to the rear, apparently completely uninterested in the proceedings and as often as not licking that particular part of her anatomy of which cats are so fond. At such times the best I could hope for was a look of patient superiority. But if a sparrow fell, in or out of her vision, it was a totally different story. She was immediately galvanised into action, knowing exactly where to search for her prize and emerging triumphantly with the bird firmly clenched between her jaws, emulating the very best of retrieving gundogs in her peculiar feline way.

The trouble was she never brought anything to hand, and when pursued would retreat to the nearest and thickest thorn bush. From there the sound of crunching bones and the odd threatening snarl would be the only sign of her appreciation. To prove her superiority as a bag filler, our blank missions were almost invariably followed by Pixie embarking on a lone foray to a nearby warren from which she seldom returned empty-handed, her set piece being to drag a dead rabbit home to parade before me with vastly exaggerated ceremony.

Nonetheless, Pixie lowered herself to accompany me on countless occasions, until she lost the ninth and last of her charmed lives beneath the wheels of the local ice-cream van on one of its regular Saturday visits. I lost simultaneously a faithful old friend and a taste for ice cream, the latter of which, curiously enough, has never returned. As my appetite for ice cream had previously been insatiable, the vendor lost one of his best customers.

My first canine companion came from a rather dubious background. Rebel, a 'black labrador' of debatable ancestry, displayed little interest in or desire to learn much of the hunting game, and seemed only intent on putting as much distance as possible between himself and anyone foolish enough to accompany him with a gun. A local trainer proffered the opinion that perhaps he had no nose for the job, but this was disproved when examining him in more detail. The nose was certainly intact, a slightly upturned proboscis protruding clearly for all to see between a pair of mischievous darting eyes; it was apparently the inability to put it to good use that somehow let him down. Being an ardent cowpat roller, perhaps it was his own aroma that was at fault, overpowering the much weaker and infinitely sweeter scent of hidden game.

Rebel's other main drawback was his inability to handle game without spoiling it. He often treated a dead pheasant as a terrier would a rat, and when bidden to retrieve would attempt to bring it to hand in small quantities, a mouthful of feathers or an odd limb on each journey. Plucking the bird was quite acceptable, but as the whole object of the exercise was to eat any game shot it was advisable to collect it oneself to prevent it from being drawn and quartered into oven-ready portions. All in all, Rebel was a failure.

Sandy, a big bouncing yellow labrador, was the next in line. In some respects he was a marked improvement over his predecessor, expressing a keen desire to hunt, flush and even retrieve game in one piece. He developed but two main faults; lack of control when hot on the heels of quarry and a distinct aversion to any water over six inches in depth – it wasn't that he was afraid to get his feet wet, but when it started creeping above his knees it was definitely time to get out.

The former habit was annoying to say the least, as any game he flushed rose much too far away. As I carried a mere twelve-bore instead of the anti-aircraft armament necessary to deal with his long-range flushes, Sandy did little to fill the game bag. His second fault could be even more distressing. Our shoot is bordered by the wide, and in parts deep, waters of the River Wensum. On frequent occasions during the game season a retrieve from water was desirable, particularly at one point at the edge of some rough marshlands where a long belt of mixed trees and thick undergrowth often provided us with a shot or two at some notoriously wild pheasants that were sometimes ejected. When flushed, the cunning old birds invariably headed across the river, and any brought down dropped either in the fast flowing waters or high and dry on the far bank. Try as I might I could never induce Sandy to leave the safety of the river bank, either by gentle encouragement, harsh commands or downright brute force, the last requiring the judicious use of a size nine wellington boot. He simply stopped wagging his tail, gave me that 'You must be joking' look and retired to watch the proceedings from a discreet distance.

One day I was really put to shame. Each few weeks during the game-shooting season my cousins, who lived nearby, invited a few guests to accompany us on our small, rough shoot. The shoot itself is rough in every meaning of the word, both in terrain and undergrowth — and the same term could be used to describe the competence of a few of those in the firing line. Soon after our arrival at the aforementioned river-side covert, a protesting cock pheasant broke out above the alder tops to curl high over my position on the river bank. To my relief it folded neatly to my shot and plummeted to earth, but as usual carried on across the river under the impetus of its own speed, bouncing with an audible thump on the grazed meadow turf. My four-legged friend, who had just suffered another acute attack of hydrophobia, sat watching it from a moderate and no doubt carefully measured distance, keeping well out of wellington boot range and making it abundantly clear that he was at present warm and dry and had every intention of so remaining.

Obeying the unwritten law of every sportsman, whose duty it is to collect and make use of every shot bird, I lowered myself into the freezing waters, first cutting a stout stick to break the ice at the water's edge and to probe a safe path across the muddy and uneven river bed. Arriving without mishap at the far bank, I collected the pheasant and began the return journey. Quite an audience had gathered to watch the display, including one large yellow labrador with a distinct smile creasing its features, waiting faithfully in a reclining posture for 'master' to return. Wading out at the edge I was almost licked to death by the uncooperative creature, much to the amusement of my fellow guns. At the very least I had expected a complimentary pat on the head for such a bold and faultless retrieve, which must have been approaching field trial standard.

Sandy was also of very limited use when in a pigeon hide. I took him decoying a few times with the idea of teaching him to pick up shot birds as they fell into the decoy pattern. He never really caught on and remained unable to discern between dead pigeons and artificial decoy birds. When a pigeon was dropped he belted from cover to retrieve the first handy object he happened to come across, whether a rubber decoy, any odd lump of wood or stone that lay in his path or, rather less frequently, the bird I had actually sent him after. He also seemed unable to grasp the fact that he could not pass through the camouflage nets I used as a hide. So now, instead of just collecting pigeons, I had the tiresome task of retrieving my hide each time he went out before shooting could again commence. I finally gave up in despair.

But to return to Trudi. When first acquired, Trudi of Freeburn appeared to lack any discipline or knowledge of what was expected of her, although her previous owner, who had recently – and very conveniently – left the country, had assured us of her suitability in the hunting field and drawn particular attention to the fact that she had earlier been employed in tracking game for a buzzard. It seemed almost too good to be true. Unfortunately it was.

He had also added, more as an afterthought once the deal had been completed, that Trudi was, as he so cautiously put it, 'a bit of a chewer'. This turned out to be a considerable understatement. A bit of a chewer? – she was more of a glutton! On her first day with us she completely demolished a pair of new shoes, gnawed a neat hole out of the kitchen table leg and chewed the top rim off her new basket. During the following week she destroyed half of the passenger seat when left alone in my van, wolfed half a pound of prime sirloin and, to cap it all, chewed the heel from one of my favourite slippers. For a while I walked around with a noticeable limp but Trudi, in her by now accomplished gastronomic manner, soon put this to rights. Two days later she gnawed the other heel down too, thus ensuring that I walked on the level.

It was the same with food. One night Trudi had a real marathon session. We had been invited to a friend's house for the evening. As usual, Barbara was in a rush to complete the housework and baking before it was time to go, and in her haste left three baking tins of hot cakes to cool on the kitchen worktop. A quick glance as we left revealed the recumbent hound lying curled up snugly in the remains of her basket by the radiator, to all appearances fast asleep and snoring loudly, or at least rendering a passable imitation of so doing. She seemed settled for the night.

Three hours later we returned home. The baking tins all stood unmoved on the worktop but now, instead of holding the grand total of 28 fresh-baked cakes, there was but one solitary bun remaining, and even that had signs of nibbling along its outer edge. Twelve mince pies, nine currant buns and three brace of shortcakes had swiftly and miraculously disappeared as if into thin air. The culprit, however, was not difficult to find. It lay in something approaching a bloated stupor, groaning and whimpering in the remains of its basket, knowing full well that it had done wrong but not knowing how its punishment would be meted out. With a resounding clang the empty bun tin collided with the skull of the sinful hound. Our gourmet retaliated with a loud belch and a succession of less polite abdominal rumblings laden with the aroma of currant buns, and heaved itself out of the back door with all the speed it could muster. But it was extremely difficult to stay angry at her for long, and when two big, round and sorrowful eyes, in a face that seemed the very picture of injured innocence, appeared out of the darkness begging for pardon, all was soon forgiven.

Even if not blessed with the grace of good or even reasonable

behaviour, Trudi was undeniably a real character and also, in spite of her unusual eating habits, maintained herself in the very peak of condition. Her short chocolate coat, described as solid liver, shone with a healthy sleekness, from the wet, enquiring nose throughout her length to the remains – also chewed – of a docked stump that passed for a tail. She was built of solid muscle, making Barbara's job all the more difficult, for it was necessary to run off as much as possible of her seemingly boundless energy before each training session could begin. As if to complete the hat trick of solids, Trudi could also be described as solid skulled, and at first was completely deaf to all commands at more than a few yards' distance. But after a few well-aimed missiles had found their mark and Trudi had acquired a comprehensive list of new and quite unprintable names, her hearing capabilities improved considerably, and apart from odd periods of 'playfulness' she began to settle down to work.

The basic requirements of a hawking dog are relatively few. All that is necessary is a steady, biddable dog which can find game, holding it 'on point' until told to flush when hawk and falconer have moved to a favourable position in readiness for the flight. Retrieving game is not necessary, or for that matter even desirable. A goshawk binds to its quarry in midair at the conclusion of a successful flight, forcing it to the ground before administering the *coup de grâce* with its strong talons, and would undoubtedly – and quite capably – contest ownership if any attempts were made to relieve it of its kill in any but the most subtle of manners. I could envisage only too well what would happen if Trudi tried to retrieve both Venom and her quarry; the results could only be a mangled hawk or a dog with an extremely sore and well-perforated nose.

Although reluctant to enter thick cover at first – one of the disadvantages of her thin coat – Trudi eventually got the message and enjoyed every opportunity of searching hedge bottom and rush bed, charging around in the manner of a brown torpedo and discovering a host of new and exciting scents of game that lurked in hiding. She also began to point game in the traditional manner of her breed, but for quite some time seemed unable to discern between legitimate game, wood mice in the hedge bottoms or a skulking heifer in a bramble patch.

The most difficult part of the operation was to instil steadiness. The pointer is of nature a wide-ranging dog, but it is neither necessary nor desirable for it to cover a full 200 square yards of ground at the same time. Indeed it is a bad fault, for when attempting to quarter such a large area the hunting dog is bound to miss the majority of hidden game; moreover, anything that is flushed should preferably be at least in sight if not in hawking range. We decided to consult the experts, who advised a check cord as the very thing with which to achieve our goal. Theoretically the check cord restricts the movements of a wayward dog, keeping it close to its handler and allowing it to hunt only the ground in the immediate vicinity, as would be ultimately required when working in cooperation with the gun or hawk. With this in mind Barbara attached a ten-yard cord to Trudi's collar in the hope it would afford her some control over the powerful beast and slow her down to Barbara's own desired rate of progress.

At that particular time Barbara weighed only a fraction over seven stones, and it proved impossible for her to restrain Trudi's forward momentum when hot on the heels of game. Trudi chased around giving a good imitation of a jet-propelled hoover when on the fresh track of a pheasant, hauling Barbara along at her own speed instead of vice versa. At least Barbara began to see much more of the countryside and to learn volumes in the art of

tracking game. Through rough hedge, thorn clump, stream and nettle bed she faithfully followed the canine tug, pausing only momentarily as the hound pointed something of interest or all too briefly answered the call of nature. It was left to me to evolve a more effective method of keeping her under some sort of control, and I did this by using a rather unorthodox form of hand signalling. Trudi was allowed to run freely beside me, but directly she strayed too far in front I stooped to pick up a clod of earth or some other suitable missile with which to reprimand her. Finally catching on to such actions, Trudi soon got the message that to see and hear was to obey, particularly when my commands were followed by a stoop to the ground. In this way she learned her first hand signal.

I began to work Trudi with the gun, hoping to give her some idea of what her training was all leading up to, though also to test her reactions when introduced to freshly killed game. It was much better than expected. When a bird was pointed, flushed and shot, instead of rushing forward as would most untrained dogs, she kept low to the ground, creeping in slowly to point the fallen quarry exactly as required. On a few occasions she crawled in rather too close, nosing the bird and nibbling out a few feathers, but at the command of 'Leave', coupled with the accustomed stoop to pick up a clod of earth, she realised it was far safer to leave all fallen game well alone.

Up until this point Trudi and Venom had been kept well and truly separated, as I was unsure whether the obvious strains of a formal introduction would upset Venom's training schedule. This proved to be a mistake, merely delaying an important step in the careers of both concerned. Although the pair were reasonably familiar at a distance, each began to view the other with a mixture of alarm and suspicion and their relationship assumed nothing more intimate than a state of armed neutrality. Trudi recognised the hawk as a flapping, screaming, nasty-tempered bundle of bells, claws and feathers, an object to be avoided at all costs. On the other hand, Venom saw the dog as a lean, wide-eyed monster that peered inquisitively into the mews window, careered around the back garden like a lunatic and periodically excavated a series of deep holes beside the weathering ground, in which for reasons best known to herself Trudi deposited the latest of a smelly collection of bones ranging from a rabbit's foreleg to the complete skull of a sheep.

When the two first met at close quarters Venom was perched on her stone block in the enclosed weathering ground, having just completed her daily bath. Trudi, after answering the call of nature (as usual in the exact centre of my path to the mews), gave herself a few minutes of vigorous exercise, charging around the lawn perimeter like a deranged greyhound hot on the heels of an invisible hare. Suddenly she stopped dead, nose to the air, tasting an unfamiliar scent that had drifted into her ever inquisitive nostrils. At the other end of the scent trail Venom remained as though carved of stone, feathers flattened, eyes bulging and wings slightly parted in readiness for flight. Trudi crept forward, nudging a wet nose towards her until it pressed against the protective wire netting of the enclosure only a matter of inches from where the hawk stood. Thus they remained for several minutes, Trudi freezing on half point and Venom boldly returning her stare. Venom's nerve proved the weaker of the two, for she suddenly bated away from the dog to the end of her leash, turning swiftly as she landed to face the creature that was no doubt close on her tail. She need not have bothered. All she saw of her suspected aggressor was a jet-propelled bundle of nerves departing in equal haste in the opposite direction. Not an auspicious beginning.

Returning to the early stages of training and the process of manning, I waited until Venom was keen and hungry before attempting to introduce them again, relying on her desire to feed to help overcome any fears of her prospective hunting companion. Trudi needed no such prompting, invariably giving the impression of being in a state of perpetual starvation, ever ready to consume an extra meal whatever the time of day. The hound was gorging herself from a large dish when I carried Venom into the kitchen, the goshawk herself being busy with a fresh rabbit leg which was in the process of being forced down her throat in alarmingly large pieces. Each was preoccupied with her meal and remained oblivious of the other's presence until I moved Venom to within a few inches of Trudi's head, which was by this time almost completely submerged in the bowl of food.

Trudi paused momentarily in her feasting – quite an event in itself — lifting her food-splattered muzzle to sniff at the juicy and rather deliciously scented rabbit leg. Venom's wings arched high and threateningly, her eyes flaring at the lowly being that had dared to interrupt her meal. Luckily with more enthusiasm than accuracy, a taloned foot guillotined forward, narrowly missing an inquisitive but hastily withdrawn nose, instead thumping on the rabbit leg. She then proceeded to give a suitably enlightening demonstration of what, given half the chance, she would doubtless do to any interfering nose if she was interrupted again, sinking her black needles repeatedly in a series of wild convulsions through the rabbit joint and into the glove. Both Trudi and my left hand needed no further convincing of the hawk's aggressive nature or of the intensity of her incredible talon power. Bolting the remains of her dinner Trudi hastily retired to the corner of the kitchen, to ponder the bird's behaviour from the safety of her usual retreat behind the door. She had lost her taste for fresh rabbit, and the pecking order had been established. There should be no cause for dispute between dog and hawk regarding ownership of any game caught.

And so it proved. At length the day arrived when our bird dog was considered to be in a fit state of mind and sufficiently obedient to be allowed the privilege of finding game for Venom. Venom had become reasonably settled in Trudi's company and displayed little sign of fear. The reverse was not true, as Trudi always remained wary of the hawk. This appeared something of an advantage, as Trudi would certainly be extra careful in her presence, fully appreciating the implications of falling foul of her majesty when food was in the offing.

With this in mind we set off for the nearest marsh; eight acres of mixed, boggy, moorhen-haunted copses, thick tangled webs of bracken and overgrown streams bordered by the grey arm of the river. Trudi, as usual, was effervescent with strength and uncontrollable vigour and had to be allowed to run wild before we reached the marsh in the hope of reducing her surplus energy. The search began in a long copse of oak, ash and tall elm trees enclosing three small weed-choked ponds of glutinous mud. The old fishponds were normally a favourite retreat of the local moorhen but although Barbara hunted Trudi back and forth through the likely hiding places we drew a complete blank, the only 'game' found being a wood pigeon that clattered noisily from the elm belt and a tawny owl disturbed from its resting place of tangled ivy. As Venom bated at it the owl glided skilfully through the trees on soundless wings but, much to its consternation, it was rapidly spotted by a cock blackbird which mobbed and cursed as it followed the night bird's path.

At the far end of the copse the marsh began, divided from the trees by a muddy drain six feet across. The banks of the drain, which during the summer months were choked with bracken and the tall flowering spikes of rosebay willowherb, had now reappeared and were almost bereft of cover. A few small patches of withered sedge overhung the water, beaten flat by the ceaseless pounding of the winds and rain, but there was scarcely sufficient cover to conceal a sparrow, let alone the much larger game that we sought. I forded the drain by a shallow bed of gravel, the stones washed clean and bright by the continual trickle of water from a deep bubbling spring upstream, progressing along the open meadow with Barbara working Trudi opposite on the far bank. A large gathering of lapwings tumbled and fell in a confused mass over the centre of the meadow, their dizzy gyrations resembling a pile of windstrewn leaves. A few birds, bolder than the rest, broke from the main bunch, arriving quickly overhead to mob and protest at the invasion of their territory. One courageous bird, spotting Venom on my fist, dived repeatedly towards her, displaying its complete mastery of the air in a flaunting manner, the wind thrumming through its pinions with the sound of tearing calico.

Trudi suddenly expressed a certain interest in a clump of dead rush growing over the water's edge and lying partly submerged below water level. She sniffed and pointed indecisively but as nothing emerged and I had already noted a row of black holes along the muddy bank, I dismissed her find as a water vole, since they were quite abundant along the water courses. Growing impatient with Trudi's indecision I signalled for Barbara to follow me upstream. Trudi reluctantly joined us but after covering 50 yards suddenly dashed back to the clump and ejected a very lively moorhen. As I watched it beat tantalisingly out of range towards the security of the river, croaking triumphantly, I cursed myself for not relying on the powers of her nose. I also received a look of patient superiority from those on the far bank. Round one to the moorhen.

We covered at least a hundred yards along the winding stream before the dog showed any further signs of interest. Here a small drainage channel trickled into the main stream and at the junction grew a bed of sedges, among which the first dark green shoots of marsh marigolds were beginning to appear. Trudi searched up and down the bank, ten yards each way, but continually returned to sniff eagerly among the tangled sedges. Encouraged by Barbara but not keen to enter the freezing depths,

she eventually slipped on the muddy bank and plunged headlong into the drain like a startled coypu, landing almost on top of an equally surprised moorhen. For a moment Venom seemed confused, but when I threw her in the wake of the departing bird she quickly picked up speed. The chase was on! The moorhen had built up a good lead and for a while it seemed as though its blurring wings would carry it safely to the nearest stretch of water but, suddenly realising the need, Venom put on a powerful burst of speed the moorhen could not hope to outfly. With a final determined lunge she snatched it from the air, the pair disappearing into a small bed of dead phragmite reeds among the shallows.

The trial run together had proved successful. Dog and handler, hawk and quarry, all had played their part. Although the flight had been relatively simple and of short duration, it had provided one of the most rewarding and satisfying experiences of our career together. The team was at last complete.

A couple of evenings later, as if to illustrate the old adage that pride comes before a fall, a state of utter pandemonium broke out in the kitchen. I had placed Venom on the wooden perching bar of her scales, which were situated in the centre of the kitchen table. Venom was watching Trudi dozing peacefully on the base of her basket after a heavy meal. Checking Venom's weight was correct, I pulled on the hawking glove ready to carry her back to the mews. Catching sight of the glove – the recognised feeding place – she bated towards it with premature hopes of her evening meal. Alas, the slit in her jesses snagged around the top bar of the scales, pulling them from the table to crash resoundingly onto the floor below, sending the pile of weights flying in all directions. Trudi leapt from her basket like a scalded cat, bounding into the adjoining hallway with her tail between her legs and skidding desperately as she fought for a grip on the polished floor tiles. Venom, also upset by the crash behind her, completed three mad circuits of the kitchen and left a trail of wreckage in her wake. Within ten seconds the place looked as though a bomb had hit it. Pictures hung drunkenly from two walls. A pot plant leaned precariously on the window sill and letters and papers were scattered far and wide, carried by the draught of her flailing wings.

A loose goshawk giving an aerobatic display around the kitchen is – even in our unusual household – at the best of times a rather unnerving experience, but when eventually recaptured between the cooking stove and the refrigerator, Venom luckily seemed none the worse for her escapade. Even Trudi eventually risked a cautious peep around the hall door. Needless to say we were subsequently banished from the kitchen and future weighing sessions took place in the comparative safety of the mews.

9

The Wild Goose Chase

Among the timeworn pages of an old falconry book I had found the fact – equally amazing and enthralling – that it was considered possible, given a particularly large and fearless female goshawk, to hunt and even catch wild geese. From the day that Venom first took prey, the thought that she might prove capable of taking such a prize was always in the back of my mind. There was a large number of geese residing in the valley – a few scattered bunches of greylags and Egyptians, but the main bulk made up of the huge Canada geese which weighed anything from nine to fourteen pounds, boasting an extended wingspan of around six feet. Quite a handful, even for the largest and bravest of goshawks.

Since taking her first moorhen Venom had not looked back, and her frequent kills supplied us with many a free meal. Pheasants, mallard, rabbits, moorhen and a host of other prey all fell foul of her flying skills. All, that was, but the geese. With them it was a different story. Indeed, the first time I managed to get her to within flying distance she refused even to try, merely looking at them in curiosity as they took to their wings honking loudly, but remaining on the glove without showing the slightest intention of giving chase. After 200 yards of patient stalking, not to mention a great deal of discomfort involved in crawling along a muddy drainage ditch to get her within range, I was somewhat disillusioned by her complete lack of interest. Could she be too well fed to try for so large a bird? Or perhaps she did not associate the geese with food? I was almost certain that she was not afraid to tackle the birds for, since her maiden flight and kill, she had always displayed a distinct readiness to try anything at least once.

I recalled the afternoon when I had cast her off ahead of me to a fallen alder trunk, ten feet off the ground, to wait for a moorhen I was hoping to drive towards her. This particular moorhen we almost knew by name, as it had delighted in causing us extreme difficulty in catching it. The wily bird spent most of its charmed life in a long rushy drain bisecting the centre of the marsh, and each time we attempted a flight the bird had an almost uncanny knack of rising from the opposite end of the drain, no matter from which direction we approached. On the day in question, hoping at last to bring the contest of wits to a successful conclusion, I cast Venom off to the tree while I walked to the opposite end of the ditch. The plan was to beat out the rushes as usual, but this time gradually working towards the hawk. If all went to plan the unsuspecting moorhen would leave the sanctuary of the rushes straight in the path of the waiting hawk. We meant to have it one way or another.

All remained quiet until I reached a point roughly half-way along the drain, when I noticed Venom suddenly stiffen and then launch herself from the lookout post. She approached the end of the drain in a fast level glide and suddenly thudded to the ground out of sight behind a stand of tall phragmite reeds. Got the bird at last! It appeared that the plan had worked and we had at last outwitted the infuriating creature. But as I approached I noticed an unusually fierce tussle was taking place between hawk and prey. Venom was fighting with a large, furry brown object that was definitely not a moorhen. Could it be a rabbit? And then I saw the long, almost hairless tail, twitching snake-like as Venom shifted her grip, and the truth suddenly dawned. To my extreme horror she was grappling with a coypu! The animal was not much bigger than a full-grown rabbit, but a coypu nonetheless, armed with a formidable set of yellow-stained incisors quite capable of chopping off her leg with one savage bite. Luckily she held it firmly by the business end, her long talons clamped around the dangerous jaws, preventing retaliation.

Solving the problem of extricating one angry goshawk from one even angrier coypu had proved a fearsome task, and it was with great relief that I eventually separated the pair. No, thinking back, even though the geese were almost three times Venom's own size and weight and it would require tremendous strength and willpower to overcome so powerful a quarry, I reassured myself that she was simply not hungry enough and decided to try her again in due course at a lower weight.

It was some time before circumstances permitted us to try again, for the geese were growing increasingly restless and were always on the move, habitually varying their feeding and resting grounds. For three days running I watched a small gaggle of seven birds grazing one of our meadows adjacent to the farmhouse. The meadow, covered only with short cattle-cropped grass and dead stands of creeping thistle, was much too open to allow a good chance of a flight, but I decided to try a cautious stalk along the thick bordering hedge of blackthorn at dusk, using the dense foliage as background cover in an attempt to blend in with the bushes in the poor light. There was an added advantage to this: Venom was always much keener at this time of the day, when she was always on the lookout for something to fill her crop for the coming night.

We entered the meadow at the end farthest from the geese by way of a small adjoining copse, taking great care to avoid the mass of dead twigs and fallen branches that lay below a row of ash trees. Half a dozen wood pigeon clattered noisily from a tall oak overhead, clapping their wings in surprise at our silent and unexpected arrival beneath them, and the rasping calls of a jay, ever watchful and alert, announced our presence in the wood. Despite clumsily ripping the seat of my trousers while having a one-sided argument with the barbed wire fence parting the copse from the meadow, a quick glance confirmed that the geese were still feeding unawares. We settled ourselves at the base of the thorn hedge, well out of sight, waiting patiently for the light to fade.

At times like this there is always plenty to occupy one's mind. A few yards away at the bottom of the blackthorns, keeping well under their protection, two full-grown rabbits were nibbling a patch of sparse turf, stopping every now and then for a cautious study of their immediate surroundings. I hoped fervently that Venom would ignore them. At the far end of the meadow where the ground dipped, a lone cormorant stood, statuesque, on the very top branch of a decayed oak tree on the bank of the lake, and overhead a huge concentration of rooks, homeward bound for their communal roost, beat rhythmically across the wide expanse of the cool, clear, evening sky.

The geese were still apparently undisturbed, feeding silently 300 yards away. One, obviously the appointed lookout, had its head held high, searching all around for any hint of danger to its little flock. Presently it too began to feed, but another bird immediately took its turn of duty, and thus they continued, ensuring nothing – and nobody – would arrive unnoticed. Catching them unawares was not going to be easy.

In due course the light began to fade, and soon all that could be seen of the geese was a row of white bellies etched against the dark background of the meadow. The time had come to begin the long, back-breaking stalk.

As we edged cautiously along the hedgerow, dodging the trailing fronds of a bramble patch, the two rabbits bolted in alarm for their burrow. Snipe rose from the boggy ground ahead, little wisps that were betrayed by their rasping calls as they rose, zigzagging, to vanish rapidly into the enveloping gloom of dusk. Pausing for a stretch and a much needed breather at the end of the covering hedge, I noted that we were just over a hundred yards from the nearest goose.

Suddenly every head went up simultaneously in positive alarm. They viewed their surroundings with suspicion, but as yet remained quiet and still. Had they seen us? One by one I watched the heads gradually lower, and soon the geese were feeding on the grass again, all but the inevitable lookout.

I now began what was to be the most difficult part of the stalk, which entailed creeping slowly towards the feeding geese on my hands and knees with Venom on my fist, using the background hedge as my only form of cover. I had taken the precaution of wearing drab, neutral-coloured clothes, but Venom's barred black and white breast would obviously not improve our chances of remaining undetected. I should also have taken the added precaution of wearing a glove on my right hand, for no sooner had I started out than my hand came into contact with something soft and clinging on the ground, a sticky and un-pleasant reminder that a herd of bullocks also grazed the meadow.

Ten agonising minutes and several cowpats later I had reached a position only 60 yards from the geese, when their leader began honking excitedly, causing the row of heads to rise once more. Soon all the birds were cackling loudly and they began to move. The geese walked slowly, but instead of retreating as expected they advanced towards us. The babel of goose talk sounded very close, ringing musically in the still atmosphere of the marsh, and I hardly dared to risk a peep for fear of putting them on the wing. But why were they coming towards us? Something else had obviously upset them. As if in answer, a yellow labrador burst through the distant hedge, where it was apparently hunting for a late pheasant among the thick scrub of brambles at the hedge bottom. The dog was plainly outlined against the darkness of the hedge, and every long neck was craned in its direction, trying to anticipate its actions and eyeing its approach with a mixture of curiosity and suspicion.

Venom was now watching the lumbering birds intently, eyes glaring, long talons gripping the gauntlet convulsively in anti-cipation of the coming fray. She crouched, ready to spring. I released the jesses as she launched herself forward, her long wing tips whipping the side of my face as she went. Travelling fast and low, hardly a foot above the ground, she kept deliberately well down to conceal her outline. Suddenly, with a great roar of wings and a bellow of urgent voices, the geese were in the air. Venom was already within ten yards, looking very small and insignifi-cant among the flailing wings of such massive birds. They rose forcefully on threshing wings, their bugling cries drowning all other sounds except the faint and to me wildly thrilling tinkle of brass hawk bells.

As Venom reached the geese she twisted rapidly in the air to pursue their departing forms. The straggling squadron approached me. Among them I could see a familiar outline, wings flickering and jesses trailing, only a matter of a few feet behind. Selecting a tail-ender she herded it from the main bunch, passing directly beside where I lay against the edge of a thistle patch and giving me an unforgettable picture of the chase as goose and hawk passed over. The goose was gaining speed, side-slipping and dodging to confuse its follower, its massive size concealing the speed of its flight. Breasting the stronger wind above the sheltering hedge behind me it lifted steeply, and Venom apparently decided that the chase was lost. She swooped down to alight in the top branches of a bare ash jutting prominently above the blackthorn, looking back for me to call her down for a reward. She was on her way as I raised my arm, braking sharply to land hard on the glove for her meal. An eventful evening; unsuccessful in terms of game, but even so, Venom had at least displayed her willingness to try to catch a goose. I felt a great step forward had been achieved in the wild goose chase.

The cold weeks of winter advanced. Venom, gaining skill and expertise from her many experiences, continued to take her toll of prey. She added a hare to the bag one frosty morning, footing it well by the head after a long flight as it bolted from a shallow form on a hill-top field of autumn barley. The hare leapt high as she snatched it in both feet, jumping and bucking fiercely in an effort to shake her off, sending great divots of earth flying in all directions. Had she taken the hare by the body it would almost certainly have kicked and sent her sprawling in the manner of a rodeo bull, but as it was she hung on bravely until the fight was over and the hare was stilled. Now, if only she could come to grips with a goose . . .

The majority of Canadas had left the area temporarily for pastures new, leaving only a handful of birds at mainly inaccessible places either on or near the lake adjoining the meadows, due to the pressures of shooting in the area. The flocks had grown increasingly warier, and the least form of disturbance would put them to flight. It was up to us to make do with lesser prey for the time being, and Venom saw to it that life was never dull.

Take the evening when we were returning home through a small wood. It had been an abnormally warm and humid day for early January, with a bright sun and gentle wind belying the fact that it was still midwinter. After hunting all the likely haunts of the local moorhen we had caught nothing, and I was about to fill Venom's crop for the night when she bated hard at something on the ground beneath a tall oak tree. Though I searched closely all I could see was a thick carpet of oak leaves, dead bracken fronds and the shrivelled remains of last summer's bed of nettles. There was no sign of life. Not prepared to let her go without some inkling of her game, I walked slowly in the general direction that attracted her. She bated again and again, each time towards a point only a few yards in front and, finally convinced she was not merely in one of her sulking moods and knowing her eyes were much sharper than mine, I let her go. Without further ado she plunged headlong into the bracken stalks, snatched with a lightning talon and hauled out a particularly large, spiny, flea-infested hedgehog. It was quickly stilled as she had the head in her paralysing grasp, before the prickly object had the time to roll itself into a defensive ball of spikes.

Once caught, however, the problem was what to do with our unusual bag. Normally we made use of everything that was taken, either to supplement Venom's diet or to grace our dinner table. This time even Venom seemed at a loss to know just how or where to tackle the spiny bundle, and I was pretty certain Barbara would not fancy hedgehog as a Sunday roast. I eventually helped Venom to make a start on her kill, as this seemed far easier than trying to separate her from her reward. My part of the bag was the sight of a swarm of hedgehog fleas leaving their benefactor as the body cooled, a fair proportion of which displayed a willing-ness to transfer their unwanted affections to me as their new host.

This was the second time in the space of a week that Venom had taken an unwanted kill. A few days before we had encoun-tered a dog stoat on the marshland border, which she took quite easily after a fast and roundabout chase in and out of the rush beds, but at least the stoat had left us with a little something to remind us of its capture. It had emptied its scent glands when caught, and for several days afterwards it was necessary to carry

Venom at arm's length, keeping well clear of the pungent, clinging aroma that stubbornly remained despite her frequent and sustained attempts to remove it in the bathtub.

Very soon we were to have one of our worst experiences together. It was while hunting a small woodland stream with Venom during a bitter spell of cold east winds and flooded marshes. We were progressing stealthily along the edge of an overflowing stream, our eyes ever watchful for the telltale ripples of a moorhen hiding under its banks, when we happened quite by accident upon a drake mallard feeding on the muddy bed of the stream with his head below the surface. He was stirring up the murky bottom of the water, probing and sifting for any delicacies enclosed within the mud. I waited for the head to rise, keeping well hidden behind the ivy draped across a fallen alder. As the head disappeared again to continue feeding, I ran forward. The result was a good close slip, not more than 20 yards, and Venom went off like a bullet to its mark.

The drake climbed forcefully through the black-barked, leafless alders, but after a short spiralling chase was taken beautifully in the air. Hawk and quarry fell to earth in a flailing of wings, but landed with a loud splash back in the brook again! Both birds hit the water bound together further upstream, with Venom still hanging grimly to the drake's back. I ran to her assistance but when I arrived both birds were completely submerged, the mallard towing Venom under the turbid floodwater in the hope of getting free. A pointed duck wing surfaced briefly from the muddy water, but disappeared just as quickly. I snatched in desperation but missed by an inch. Eventually the drake's head popped up among a patch of weed at the near edge for a quick breather, and luckily I managed to grab it before it submerged again, enabling me to lift it clear of the water. On the end hung a goshawk – a dripping wet, muddy, evil-smelling goshawk, her eyes glaring red and her streaked breast heaving with her efforts.

I was rather surprised when she allowed me to take her hard-won prize with scarcely a struggle, but when she began to shiver and wheeze and stood awkwardly on the glove I became filled with remorse. She was obviously waterlogged and very cold. The icy blast was still cutting relentlessly from the east, which made matters worse, for I had nearly a full mile to cover over open ground to reach the van, with Venom fully exposed to the bitter elements. I opened my windproof jacket and held her inside. She accepted this unusual position with complete indifference, which only served to make me more anxious about her condition. When we eventually reached the comparative shelter of the van I placed her gently on the passenger seat and offered food. She showed no sign of interest. Before the epic struggle she had been very keen and hungry, but now expressed little desire to eat, still shuddering and spluttering violently with the effects of the freezing water. I must dry her out, and quickly.

As luck would have it we were not far from home and it was only a matter of minutes before she was placed on a stone block in front of a roaring fire, while I played the hair dryer on the matted feathers of her back to speed up the process. Gradually she began to perk up and take notice, as her feathers started to recover some of their former fluffiness. She stood up boldly on the block, roused her feathers and then bated hard from the whirring hairdryer as if noticing it for the first time. This was more like Venom.

I fetched a fresh rabbit leg from the game larder and she snatched it ungracefully from my fingers, mantling over it fiercely as she began to feed. Ten minutes later only the bone remained and Venom, after stropping her beak to clean it on the rough stone, drew up one leg into her flank feathers and fluffed out her drying plumage, looking around in amazement as if puzzled by all the fuss. But just to be on the safe side I left her in the warmth of the sitting room for the rest of the afternoon.

Soon there were only three weeks of the wildfowling season left and, as we had progressed no further in our quest for a Canada goose, my hopes gradually receded with each passing day. But then one morning my prayers were answered. As I drove past the meadows in the early morning light, the lush greenness in places covered with a powdering of snow, I glanced briefly at the old haunts of the geese. I could hardly believe my eyes. There, no more than 200 yards from the roadside, a huge army was assembled – a hundred and fifty Canada geese!

The pack had divided into two main groups, one of about 80 birds feeding on a clear patch of grass only a short distance from the farmhouse and the other, slightly less in number, grazing contentedly in the centre of the marsh. A few odd stragglers fed along the banks of a shallow drain between the two groups, and were joined from the lake by a pair of Egyptian geese, smaller and more brightly clad in a mixture of pinks and browns, which stood out plainly against their more soberly clad companions at the breakfast table. The smallest bunch of Canadas were almost within flying range of a deep drainage ditch, which at most held only a foot of water, providing ideal cover along which to attempt a stalk. I could hardly wait for the coming of dusk.

The geese left their feeding ground in late morning for a wash and brush-up on the lake, but fortunately returned in the afternoon for another helping of the meadow grass. A small flock drifted down to alight in the same position as those on our last attempt, and I decided to try them using the same line and method of approach. We managed to creep to within 60 yards without too much trouble or discomfort, but as we crawled along the drain it was clear from their behaviour that the geese were restless and unsure of their safety in the half-light of dusk. An added nuisance was the patches of brittle ice lining each bank of the ditch, forcing me to wade along the centre to avoid the giveaway crackle of breaking ice. The water was deeper there, almost two feet. My boots were only eighteen inches high, with the inevitable result that my legs felt as though they had been severed at the knee, numbed and frozen by the icy water. Soon we encountered an even worse obstacle. Further along a thin skin of ice covered the complete width of the drain. It was impassable. I peeped cautiously over the bank. Still at least 40 yards from the nearest goose but unable to approach further, I cast Venom forward.

At first she appeared to ignore the geese completely, sweeping almost lethargically in a wide circle well downwind of the flock, but suddenly, summoning a spurt of energy, she hurtled towards them to attack. This time she meant business. Sixty huge birds rose as one, with desperation and panic in their ringing voices. A single goose remained on the grass, twisting, flapping and tumbling as it fought to escape a vice-like grip. Venom clung to it bravely, sometimes on top, at others beneath, as the pair contested for the upper hand. She had taken the goose by the base of its long neck, but by slashing her repeatedly across the head with its powerful wings the bird forced her to relinquish her grasp, and it escaped, beating a hasty retreat towards the lake and calling loudly as it flew.

Bitter with the knowledge of such a narrow defeat, I hauled myself from the freezing water and squelched across the grass to take her back on the glove. Venom was panting heavily with her exertions but, apart from an obvious blow to her pride, she was apparently otherwise unhurt. Her widened eyes flared madly as she gripped the glove convulsively at the memory of her first contact with the goose. On the short turf at my feet lay a handful of buff-grey feathers, a meagre reward for such a brave flight. I fed her well, hoping to retain a definite relationship between the geese and food. Maybe next time we would succeed, or the time after? I could be certain of only one thing. If Venom was to catch and hold a goose it would take all her reserves of strength and spirit to overcome such a powerful quarry.

A gooseless week passed. It was not lack of trying that made Venom fail in two more attempts; both times it was due to circumstances beyond control. On the first occasion she was nearly within striking distance of a party of 40 geese when a moorhen rose from their ranks and was taken easily in a rolling glide. Totally addicted to these birds, Venom had the rather annoying habit of ignoring all else when one came in sight. Although legions of geese erupted all around her at close range, she took not the slightest notice once she had seen the moorhen. The following evening a jet fighter from a nearby airbase shattered the silence, roaring low across the evening sky with its neon lights winking red and green in the dusk, putting the geese to flight long before they offered us a chance.

It was becoming increasingly difficult to approach the restless geese, for they had learned their lesson only too well. If Venom was even so much as glimpsed on my fist the area was cleared in a matter of seconds as they hurriedly dispersed to the sanctuary of the lake and river.

Time was running out and my hopes were low. Then came the night of the gales. Following a fierce scarlet sunset a gentle breeze began to feather the tops of the tallest elms and, as night advanced, grew in force to a raging gale, playing havoc with anything and everything that attempted to block its path. By midnight trees were falling continually as if pushed by some giant's hand, tiles cascaded from the house roof with monotonous regularity and the bales of a strawstack near the garden, half a hundredweight in each, were picked up effortlessly to be swept and tossed across the fields and along the lanes like a trail of autumn leaves. As a safety measure I took Venom from the mews, which was fully exposed to the brunt of the gale, bringing her indoors to spend a comparatively quiet night in the spare bedroom.

For most of the long night I lay unable to sleep, listening all the time to the unearthly sounds of the raging gale, its most powerful bursts often accompanied by the banging and thumping of some unknown piece of wreckage as it was hurled past the house. Electricity and telephone services were soon put out of action, reducing us to the flickering, uncertain light of two candles, as poles carrying the cables were snapped like matchwood or demolished in the wooded areas by falling trees. This was indeed a nightmare come true.

By first light, luckily, the wind had decreased in force and we were able to assess the extent of the damage. To say it was colossal would have been a gross understatement. Tiles lay scattered and broken beneath the eaves of the house, trees had been uprooted in almost every exposed hedgerow and Trudi's kennel – fortunately unoccupied – was standing drunkenly in the middle of the vegetable patch next door. In the nearby woods a path of trees had fallen like a huge deck of cards, massive trunks that had been formed over decades and shattered in minutes, unable to stand the immense strain of the wind. All roads from the village were blocked by fallen trees, the worst hit being sealed off by over a score of tall firs.

On the marsh little had changed except for the loss of one or two trees in the more exposed areas. A mixed raft of tufted duck, pochard and coot bobbed sickeningly on the choppy waters of the lake like a flotilla of corks and, keeping well under the protection of a tall sand bank, 50 or so geese sheltered head to wind, waiting patiently for the gale to subside. By midafternoon it still showed little sign of abating. The geese were forced to venture out to the open meadow to graze. The only sheltered piece of the pasture was along the lee side of a thick copse and it was to there that the birds moved to feed in earnest, barely 40 yards from the nearest cover. With hope renewed I ran back to the house to collect Venom. This was our big chance.

The cover of the copse allowed us to approach the geese more closely than ever before, and following a relatively easy approach we gained the sanctuary of a dense holly thicket, now denuded of its berries by the flock of fieldfares that broke out as we advanced. It seemed so quiet and still in the copse, which was sheltered from the wind by a wide belt of blackthorns. The tops of the taller ash trees still thrashed wildly high above us, but where we crouched concealed only a faint breeze managed to penetrate the bushes.

Venom seemed reluctant to fly at first despite encouragement, sizing up the situation from the glove very carefully before committing herself to flight. Suddenly, her mind made up, a definite change of attitude came over her and she launched powerfully into the attack. As she burst from cover with the wind singing through her pinions, 50 long necks rose in unison, at once recognising the familiar barred grey shadow that was bearing down upon them. The flock lifted into the air but Venom kept purposefully low, selecting her target carefully from the mass of flailing wings. She passed beneath the main bunch with the speed of a bullet, and then she lunged upwards.

The suddenness of the attack took some of the geese by complete surprise. Before they had fully realised the danger, she had arrowed between the wings of the nearest goose, and took it with both talons outstretched. Both birds spun heavily to earth in a flailing bundle of wings, leaving a small puff of feathers hanging momentarily in the air above them, to be swept away by the next gust of wind. A desperate struggle began. Could Venom hold so large a bird? She appeared to have both talons firmly locked but the goose was fighting hard. It tumbled, rolled and jumped, thrashing her soundly with its heavy wings and towing her dizzily across the grass, but still she held on boldly. Almost breathless, I reached the scene a few moments later and dived for a hold. We had done it at last!

Collapsing on the grass beside them, panting heavily with the excitements and thrills of such a desperate fight, I looked across at Venom, now mantling fiercely astride her massive quarry. Having always been one who saw to her food above all else, she quickly roused her battered plumage into order and began to pluck the bird aggressively, spreading her wings to protect the coveted prize. The ground was soon littered with feathers, mainly from the goose, but mingled with them were a few heavily barred ones from Venom's breast. Savouring the moment, I allowed her to feed contentedly until her crop was almost bursting. Venom had certainly earned her reward.